Presenting Data Effectively

Presenting Data Effectively

Communicating Your Findings
for Maximum Impact

Stephanie D. H. Evergreen

Evergreen Data & Evaluation, LLC

Los Angeles | London | New Delhi
Singapore | Washington DC

Los Angeles | London | New Delhi
Singapore | Washington DC

FOR INFORMATION:

SAGE Publications, Inc.
2455 Teller Road
Thousand Oaks, California 91320
E-mail: order@sagepub.com

SAGE Publications Ltd.
1 Oliver's Yard
55 City Road
London EC1Y 1SP
United Kingdom

SAGE Publications India Pvt. Ltd.
B 1/I 1 Mohan Cooperative Industrial Area
Mathura Road, New Delhi 110 044
India

SAGE Publications Asia-Pacific Pte. Ltd.
3 Church Street
#10-04 Samsung Hub
Singapore 049483

Acquisitions Editor: Helen Salmon
Assistant Editor: Katie Guarino
Editorial Assistant: Kaitlin Coghill
Production Editor: Stephanie Palermini
Copy Editor: Janet Ford
Typesetter: C&M Digitals (P) Ltd.
Proofreader: Christine Dahlin
Indexer: Joan Shapiro
Cover Designer: Chris Metzner and
                              Gail Buschman
Marketing Manager: Nicole Elliott

Printed in the United States of America

Library of Congress Cataloging-in-Publication Data

Evergreen, Stephanie D. H.

Presenting data effectively : communicating your findings for maximum impact / Stephanie D. H. Evergreen, Evergreen Data & Evaluation, LLC.

pages cm
Includes bibliographical references and index.

ISBN 978-1-4522-5736-5 (pbk. : alk. paper)
ISBN 978-1-4833-1218-7 (web pdf)

1. Visual communication. 2. Presentation graphics software. 3. Graphic design (Typography) 4. Information visualization. I. Title.

P93.5E94 2014
001.4'226—dc23   2013022115

This book is printed on acid-free paper.

15 16 17 10 9 8 7 6 5 4 3

Brief Contents

Detailed Contents

3 Type

4 Color 91

5 Arrangement 123

6   A Short Last Word on Presenting Data Effectively   163

Appendix   173

Index   179

Effective Data Presentation Mediums

Icons identify places in the book where I discuss reports, slideshows, posters, and graphs, respectively. Readers can find discussion of each specific medium on the page numbers below:

Reports

3, 24, 28, 29, 40, 42, 48, 59, 63, 66, 67, 69, 75, 76, 79, 80, 83, 84, 95, 98, 107, 109, 125, 132, 134, 139, 143, 151, 152, 167

Slideshows

4, 22, 30, 34, 38, 42, 66, 67, 71, 78, 84, 94, 105, 110, 112, 137, 139, 146, 165, 167

Posters

6, 33, 34, 74, 77, 111, 127, 131, 134

Data Displays

8, 48, 50, 85, 92, 98, 112, 124, 142, 153

Online

2, 16, 18, 24, 29, 31, 36, 37, 44, 46, 47, 50, 53, 54, 70, 78, 88, 98, 100, 102, 105, 106, 113, 120, 125, 130, 137, 138, 139, 149, 159, 168, 170

About the Author

 Stephanie Evergreen is a well-known speaker, designer, and evaluator who brings a research-based approach to helping clients polish and enhance their work. She is the owner of Evergreen Data, a data presentation consulting firm, and holds a PhD in interdisciplinary evaluation. Her dissertation focused on the extent of graphic design use in written research reports. Prior to starting her own consulting firm, Stephanie spent 5 years at the internationally recognized Evaluation Center at Western Michigan University. Within the American Evaluation Association, Stephanie founded a topical interest group on data visualization and reporting and led the Potent Presentations Initiative, the largest known movement by a professional association to improve the quality of conference presentations. Stephanie is coeditor and coauthor of two issues of *New Directions for Evaluation* on data visualization. She regularly blogs on data presentation issues at stephanieevergreen.com/blog. When not engaged as a speaker and consultant on presenting data effectively, Stephanie lives in Kalamazoo, Michigan.

Acknowledgments

When Helen Salmon, my editor at Sage, contacted me to ask if I would consider a book on the growing field of information design and effective data presentation, I had just finished my dissertation; I hadn't even graduated yet. At first, I couldn't imagine it—I thought my dissertation had zapped my entire reserves of blood, sweat, and tears. But, the following special people convinced me that this book was necessary (they were right) and helped shape the environment to get me here.

Family

Byce Evergreen

Jeff Evergreen

Tina Higdon

Mike Higdon

Paula Miller

John Easley

Colleagues

Stuart Henderson, catalyst

Chris Metzner, provided art for the cover and interior

Chris Coryn

Mary Piontek

Cynthia Phillips

Nancy Mansberger

Peter Brakeman

Kevin Brady

Christy Kloote

Susan Kistler and the American Evaluation Association

Sage

Helen Salmon

Kaitlin Coghill

Those individuals who granted permission for me to highlight their work.

The thorough and kind reviewers listed below:

Courtney E. Cole, Ohio University

Jessica Crowe, University of North Texas at Dallas

Rosalyn M. King, Northern Virginia Community College and Capella University

Lois Linden, College of Saint Mary

Diana Linn, Texas A&M International University

Jonathan Lord, University of Salford

Jennifer S. Perkins, Walden University

Gary L. Reglin, Adjunct professor at Nova Southeastern University and retired professor of educational leadership at University of West Florida

Jennifer L. Thompson, The Chicago School of Professional Psychology

CHAPTER 1

The Justification for Presenting Data Effectively

Learning Objectives

After reading this chapter, you will be able to:

- Contrast weak and effective data presentation
- Articulate the basic steps of how the brain retains information
- Pinpoint where in that process the graphic design cues are useful
- Position data presentation within the web of related fields

When you need to convince your colleagues that their data presentations need a bit of sprucing up, then this is the chapter to surreptitiously place in their mailboxes. This chapter discusses why it is so critically important for us to learn about better data presentation. You probably already know some of this intuitively. For example, you were bored during a presentation as the speaker reads the text off his slides; or you struggled to keep alert while dragging through a report and peeked ahead at how many more pages of narrative await you; or you wasted time trying to decode a cluttered graph and your eyes glazed over.

As a speaker and author, the eye glaze is like the kiss of death. When you see it happening to members of your audience, you know that you have 3 . . . 2 . . . 1 . . . yes—an audience checking their email messages. Whichever end of the exchange you are on, you understand the importance and necessity of a presentation that attracts and maintains interest.

Dissertation in a Nutshell

I looked at the extent of graphic design use in evaluation reports, which I gathered from a national repository. With an extensive literature review of cognition-based design theory, and the iterative input of a panel of graphic design experts, I pulled together a checklist of graphic design best practices, as applied to the context of evaluation and research reports. A version of the checklist can be found in the appendix of this book and is downloadable in the online companion.

I trained a group of raters and then asked them to apply the checklist to a culled sample of the evaluation reports. The results probably will not surprise you too much. The reports scored high on those checklist items that are default settings found in most word-processing programs.

The reports scored lowest on the presence of graphics. Graphics, in this case, refers to pictures, diagrams, charts, or graphs. Yes, some reports had no graphs at all. Others that continued to rely on default settings produced cluttered and miscolored graphs that cause confusion for readers.

In fairness, there were actually several reports that really got it right and produced engaging materials that lured the readers to scroll through, regardless of report length.

So, those were the main findings of the study, but in the process of conducting it we discovered something else: We used interrater reliability to look at how closely the trained raters matched my scoring of the sampled reports. The score was high. In other words, with some training and maybe a splash of predisposed interest, people can learn what great (and not-so-great) data presentations look like. Some folks like to claim that I have some innate talent or creativity, but I do not think that is true. It can be learned. You can do it, too.

Consequently, how is it that most of us can relate to the irritation of sitting through weak data presentations, but there is still so much weak data presentation in the world? Well, old habits are hard to break. Many of us who come up through an academic pipeline have been drilled with our department's required style manuals, which seemed to point toward pages and pages of prose, or the painful construction and formatting of graphs and figures. In turn, some of us found our way to government positions where PowerPoint templates and colors were mandated, and clearance departments had a final say in the look of all reports. And for most of us, we are better at critiquing bad design than envisioning how an effective data presentation looks. This book is your new style guide, your step-by-step resource on how to make your work more memorable. But don't worry—these steps are still aligned with the major academic style guides and with the U.S. government's guidelines around universal accessibility. We're good to go. So, let's go.

What Does Effective Data Presentation Look Like?

It seems that it is always easier to spot weak presentations than to organically develop effective data presentation. It may be useful to walk through a few examples.

Reports

FIGURES 1.1 and 1.2   Cover and second page of a weak report

DEATH BY BOREDOM: THE ROLE OF VISUAL PROCESSING THEORY IN WRITTEN
EVALUATION COMMUNICATION

Stephanie D. H. Evergreen, Ph.D.

Western Michigan University, 2011

Evaluation reporting is an educational act and, as such, should be communicated using principles that support cognition. This study drew upon visual processing theory and theory-based graphic design principles to develop the Evaluation Report Layout Checklist intended to guide report development and support cognition in the readers of evaluation reports. It was then reviewed by an expert panel and applied by a group of raters to a set of evaluation reports obtained from the Informal Science Education evaluation website with maximum variability sampling. Results showed fairly high exact percent agreement and strong to very strong correlation with the author's ratings. Ratings revealed a low level of theory-based report formatting in use of graphics and some aspects of type, alignment, and color among evaluation reports in the sample.

TABLE OF CONTENTS

Familiar, isn't it? If you haven't guessed, we are looking at the first two pages of a report. Indeed, the first page is pulled exactly from my dissertation. I followed the university's dissertation formatting guidelines with precision—and if you have ever been in a similar situation you know that at times the guidelines can appear more mysterious than the study itself. On examination, there are several elements that actively prevent a reader from engaging with the text. The title, for example, is set in all caps, which makes it difficult to read at length (and aren't they all lengthy?). The centered alignment adds another layer of reading difficulty. Then when the reader whips past the first page to get to the content, they are met with, well, the table of contents (pages of them, in my case). Page numbers are misaligned. It is a mess. With just these first two pages, the reader now understands that if she chooses to continue to read, making any sense or meaning is going to take a bit of work. Ultimately, this type of reporting does not engage the reader. It is weak. Now, let's contrast that a bit.

Notice any changes? Of course you do! While I left some of the healthy white space on the cover page of the weaker version, I added a photograph of a bored child. At a glance, the photograph is interesting, engaging to a viewer, relatable, and works hard to communicate the author's point. Now, I understand that a graduate college never allows a dissertation submission with a photograph on the cover. But then again, few people outside of the

FIGURES 1.3 and 1.4   Cover and second page of an effective report

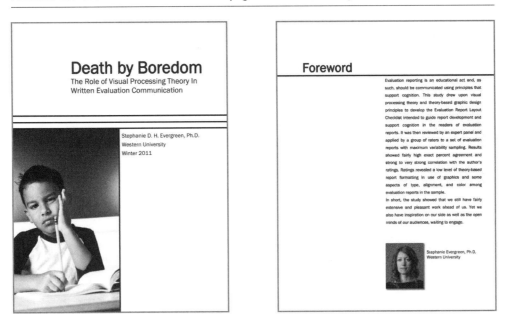

graduate college, and an applicant's advisors, even read the dissertation in the condition it is submitted. For outside audiences, adopt the flexibility to repackage the study to make it more appealing, interesting, and memorable. As we discuss later on, graphics are a great way to do just that.

Notice that the title is larger rather than in all caps. It stands out as the most important text on the page and is now more legible. The subtitle was bumped down to its own line. On the second page, I replaced the table of contents with a slightly more intriguing foreword. It is short, increasing the likelihood that people read it, and it contains the personal touch of my picture.

If you had the choice to flip through either of these reports over your lunch break, I feel certain that you would pick the effective one.

Slideshows

Of course, this range of quality data presentation happens in all types of dissemination formats. Home slides like this one are pretty common fare.

It is likely that you instantly recognize this design as a slide template, one of the default options that come preloaded in slide software programs. Communicating "default" is probably not what we seek when we are trying to engage an audience with our work. On close inspection, you notice that there is also a bit of uneven spacing happening in the chunk of text at the bottom of the cover slide. The company logo is somewhat plastered in the upper right corner. The font, as we discuss later, is inappropriate for slide projection.

FIGURES 1.5 and 1.6   First and second slide from a weak slideshow

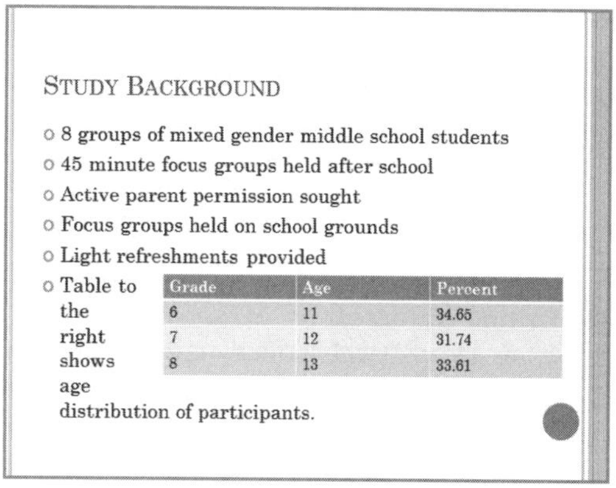

On the interior slide, shown on the right, there is simply too much text. The table is full of numbers that take a lot of cognitive processing to understand. The alternating banded rows further impact legibility. Imagine trying to weed through this slide while the speaker is reiterating the points verbally. This is a great way to lose an audience by just the second slide of a talk. How could these slides work better?

FIGURES 1.7 and 1.8   First and second slide from an effective slideshow

In this version, a large relatable image draws in the viewer on the home slide. It gives a much clearer indication about the subject of the presentation to audience members milling around the room before they find their seats. Obvious information (like the name of the conference and the date of the presentation) are removed to declutter the slide. The font is larger, and the sans serif style is much easier on the eyes, particularly when projected.

The interior slide now visualizes the logistical description that had been text-based in the weak slides in a better manner. The diagram communicates in an instant what the table did not. At this point it looks as if critical details, such as the fact that the focus groups were mixed gender and that we served snacks, are gone, but they really are not. It is just that those details come from the speaker, who is the proper center of attention. Effective data presentation with a deck of slides means that the visuals are a support tool, not a replacement for the speaker.

Posters

I would wager that once or twice you wandered the aisles of a conference poster exhibit and spotted some posters that are similar to the example below.

FIGURE 1.9 Weak research poster

Research posters are usually at least 3.5 feet wide and 3.5 feet tall. The poster shown here has been shrunk to the extent that you can't read the text. But you are familiar with the general layout of a poster where narrative text is used to explain the background, literature review, methods, analysis, and discussion of a study. Posters are usually intended to stand alone and to deliver the entire message without a speaker to elaborate. Yet this poster cannot explain the study because it is impeding efforts to engage and communicate.

While relevant to the topic, the background picture obscures the text and renders it somewhat illegible. Imagine trying to read the text that rests on top of the principal's patterned tie. The average conference-goer will not even bother. The table covering the principal's face is also oddly placed and with its white background, it is a literal bright spot to a viewer, sticking out more so than anything else on the poster. The table's encapsulation inside a box further contributes to its prominence. With this level of emphasis, whatever is in that table better be the key take-home message.

Research posters are difficult to master. Poster designers often have to balance the competing needs of large text that is readable at a distance and when standing close. The poster size itself allows for much more space than we are used to in a research paper, and thus compels a desire to add some visual interest. At play are also poster guidelines dictated by the conference, such as a minimum font size. Now, mix in the tendency to want to detail the entire contents of the related research paper, and that is how we end up with posters like the above example. Still, it is possible to work within all of those parameters to develop a more effective data presentation.

FIGURE 1.10 Effective research poster

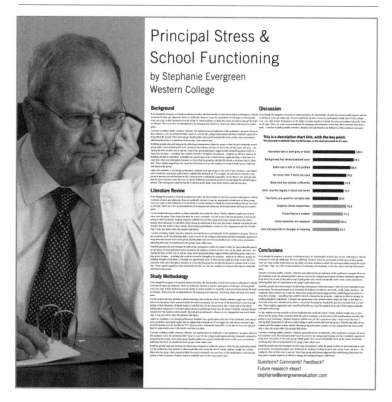

Creating this version of the poster required very few changes. It uses the same fonts, font size, and photograph of a disheartened principal, yet carries out the key message more clearly. Good poster design can and should incorporate some visual imagery; it just should not hide behind text. Here, it is off to one side, resulting in a better view of both the photograph and the text. Rather than a table, which feels a bit like it is just more text, the revised poster includes a graph of the key findings. However, the size of the photograph and the graph mean that some of the poster's space is no longer available for the study narrative; that is okay. There is still plenty of space to relay most necessary details for an onlooker to comprehend the study procedures.

Data Displays

We have one more comparison to make here before we've rounded out the set. Let's look at data displays, since they tend to make an appearance in each of the previous methods of presentation.

If you were anywhere near the discussions around data visualization in the past few years then you know that pie charts are a bit of a flashpoint. Some people think that there is no better way to express parts of a whole. Other people assert that pie charts are fairly useless because humans are pretty terrible at judging area. Of course, that specific problem is compounded by rendering the pie chart in three dimensions. Research in this area is quite clear—three-dimensional data displays slow down interpretation and often lead to inaccurate comprehension. In addition, though this book is printed in just two colors, the original display used the default color scheme of Microsoft Excel, where each slice of the pie is assigned a different color. How well do the distinctive colors hold up in the color scheme of this book? Many organizations save on costs by printing in black and white, which means that we will have to devise more effective data presentation methods.

FIGURE 1.11   Weak data display (3D pie chart)

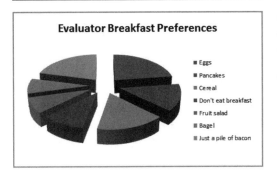

Source: © 2012 Reprinted with permission from the American Evaluation Association.

Several adjustments make this same data display more effective. I represented the data by a bar chart instead of a pie chart because humans are much better at roughly assessing length than they are at perceiving area. Bar charts are easier to decode. I also ordered the bars from the greatest to the least to make that decoding process even more straightforward. The graph now has a more descriptive title and an explanatory subtitle. In a sense, I have taken a stance on the analysis in the study, created a story to tell. Previously, in the weak example, the data were simply presented. Even if the study authors had an opinion, it was left up to the viewer to interpret the data and decide what was important. The problem with presenting data in that manner is that it assumes that the average viewer takes the time to engage with the data and to pull out the most pertinent elements. That is quite a large assumption. Communication with our stakeholders is clearer and more effective when we highlight the graph's key points. The viewer can always disagree and the remainder of the data is there with which to do so; nothing is hidden. This format just respects the time and energy of the audience and relays the data directly. In the effective example, the key message is both stated in the title and made obvious by changing the bar colors such that the less important points are a light gray and the point that illustrates my message pops out the most.

Regardless of the field, position, or geographic location, we are all in the business of presentation. The way we package our words and our data is reflected in our audience's perceptions

FIGURE 1.12   Effective data display (bar chart ordered greatest to least)

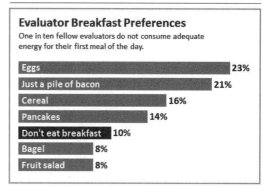

Source: © 2012 Reprinted with permission from the American Evaluation Association.

of our quality, credibility, and trustworthiness. These four sets of examples reflect the obvious differences and stark contrast between weak and effective data presentation. Everyone is tired of the current models of data presentation precisely because they are weaker and do not engage viewers, or increase their chances at recalling the information presented. Effective data presentation creates a shortcut to audience comprehension.

What Makes Data Presentation *Effective?*

This section may be the most important part of the entire book. We are going to devote some space here to describe the science of communication. Often, my workshop participants, full of excitement and inspiration, try to take fresh ideas back to their home organizations and universities and no one listens; someone says something like "we don't have time to worry about making things pretty." One workshop attendee who worked in academia said that if a faculty member does not use bullet points and text-heavy slides, she is seen as unprofessional and unscientific. By far, this resistance from the uninitiated is one of the most common areas of concern for my workshop participants. It is about discussing data in ways that align with how the human brain operates and how people retain information. If our hard work is to draw attention, make an impact, and convince others to take action (e.g., award funding), then communication can no longer be presented in the weak style of the status quo. An effective data presentation may look pretty, but the true goal is to support audience cognition.

Visual processing theory describes the way the brain perceives and interprets what the eyes see. Graphic design incorporates the science of visual perception, to create designs that better attract viewer attention. What follows is a supremely oversimplified primer on visual processing theory, how information ultimately gets retained in the mind of an audience member, and how effective data presentation assists in that retention process.

Pictorial Superiority Effect

Rather than delay the suspense, let's jump right to the main point: we primarily get our information about the world through our eyes. Certainly, we have other sensory organs that feed information to our brains. But the reality is that vision dominates. Today's researchers refer to this as the pictorial superiority effect, a term so difficult to work into a conversation that it clearly came from academia. The pictorial superiority effect essentially reminds us that what the eyes see always wins, even if we intentionally try to confuse our senses. Large parts of our brain and brain activity are devoted to visual processing (Stenberg, 2006).

FIGURE 1.13   The pictorial superiority effect essentially means our brains are led by our eyes

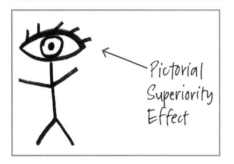

The following is an illustrative story: When I was in fourth grade, we had to devise an experiment for our school science fair. I ran a taste test experiment, where I poured three identical glasses of cola. I left one glass as is, dropped red food coloring into the second glass to give it a red tint, and added green food coloring to the third glass. Then I called my friends over and made them taste each glass (this was before concerns about the potential germ proliferation caused by sharing glasses). Across the board, my friends thought that the red cola was cherry flavored and the green cola was disgusting. What the eyes see always wins, even though scent and taste should have made the experiment obvious.

This example is not just fourth-grade foolishness, either. In his book *Brain Rules,* John Medina retells how French researchers at the University of Bordeaux conducted a similar experiment on a more sophisticated set of subjects, wine sommeliers, which must be the best job in the whole world. Wine sommeliers are the people who judge wine competitions. However, it is not easy to become a wine sommelier. There are dense textbooks to study and challenging tests to pass that assess learned knowledge about wine and wine history and determine the extent of the sensitivity of the tester's palette. Wine sommeliers have extremely well-refined smell and taste abilities. These people can detect that a peach orchard was growing 200 years before the vineyard was planted on the same grounds. They can actually pick up the peach flavor and aroma in the wine. As an acknowledgment of their talents, they wear a special pin on their lapels identifying their superhuman powers. It's amazing. Anyway, back to the study where the researchers at the University of Bordeaux (right!) obtained white wine and tinted it red with dyes and food coloring. Then they gave it to the wine sommeliers. You can probably guess what happened. When the wine sommeliers were asked to describe the wine to the researchers, even though their noses and mouths were screaming "white wine! white wine!", they used the language of red wine in their descriptions. Vision wins.

The pictorial superiority effect is exactly what we can use to our advantage in effective data presentation. This effect is what allows us to move information along the memory continuum to catch the reader's eye, focus the reader's attention, and affix in the reader's memory. Let's talk about how the pictorial superiority effect works in three stages along the memory continuum.

Early Attention

As far as anyone knows, this visual dominance has always been a human trait (except, of course, in cases of individuals who are blind at birth). To a large extent, it is this effect that has advanced our survival as a species to date. Humans are naturally skilled at scanning the horizon, looking for food, or mates, or danger. We are adept at noticing patterns in our environment and spotting abnormalities of those patterns.

FIGURE 1.14   We have always had the pictorial superiority effect

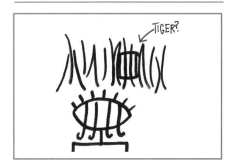

In fact, we are so awesome at using our eyes to take in information, our brains do not even have to be cognitively engaged for the process to work. When something just catches our eye, it is tapping into our earliest stages of attention, an activity that is so subtle that some researchers call this stage *pre*-attention (Callaghan, 1989; Ware, 2013). This process occurs without focused energy on the part of the viewer.

Effective data presentation makes use of this early attention function.

A lot of graphic design operates in this stage. Emphasis techniques like color, alignment, motion, orientation, and size grab a viewer's early attention. Visual cognition research reveals that capitalizing on the pictorial superiority effect boosts the audience's ability to recall information. However, in order to be able to recall information, it must be stored in the brain's long-term memory, which is Stage 3. The path that moves information from Stage 1, early attention, to Stage 3, long-term memory, can be a bit tricky, but graphic design helps it get there.

FIGURE 1.15   We can apply the pictorial superiority effect to our research reporting

Working Memory

Now to discuss the tricky part of that path—working memory.

Working memory is what we use when something has caught our eye and we decide to bring it into mental focus, to contemplate it, and to engage our cognitive energy. Working memory is where we wrestle with information to understand and process it so that it can

FIGURE 1.16 Avoiding the overload of working memory is a key tenet behind effective design choices

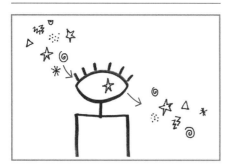

FIGURE 1.17 Organizing information makes it easier to comprehend

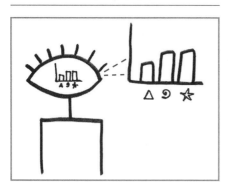

eventually be assimilated into long-term memory; but the problem is that working memory is like a sieve. It is weak, can't wrestle for long, and can't wrestle with much. Research shows we only hold 3–5 chunks of information in working memory at any one time, and that number even varies by the environmental context (Baddeley, 1992; Cowan, 2000; Xu & Chun, 2006). If a subject is in a stressful or distracting atmosphere, even 3 chunks of information cannot be handled at once. When a viewer's working memory is overloaded, it drops some chunks of information, and then misunderstanding or frustration results (Woodman, Vecera, & Luck, 2003).

Enter graphic design. Although working memory has limits on its cognitive load, graphic elements can reduce the overload by doing some of the thinking for the reader. By visually organizing and emphasizing information, graphic design makes it more accessible for the reader, increasing the capacity to engage with the words and data.

By virtue of this process, richer chunks of information are actually created, which in turn enables the viewer to essentially handle a larger cognitive load at one time (Shah, Mayer, & Hegarty, 1999). Paying attention to format, color, and font choices assists readers in encoding our information and grappling with it; this is how comprehension occurs. The more engagement, the more that passes through the working memory checkpoint, the more information that stays in long-term memory.

Long-Term Memory

The last stage is long-term memory. When information is received into long-term memory, it can be recalled later on, retold to others, and combined with other ideas—to evolve into something even more amazing.

In order for new information to be encoded in the brain, it must be incorporated into existing schemas. If you are like me, you probably have not heard the phrase "existing schemas" since high school biology class. This phrase refers to our mental models or our belief systems about how the world works. Again, effective data presentation assists this process because graphics are particularly good at activating those existing schemas. When we add visuals to verbal explanations, readers generate 65% more creative transfer and applications of knowledge (Mayer, 1997). That is why so many of us are better at remembering faces than names, and at navigating using landmarks rather than street names. We are visual beings.

Now, there are a host of other factors that help us retain information for the long haul. We have probably all been in situations where we remembered something for 2 days only to forget it after 2 months. Individual experiences, culture, emotion, and even exercise can play into the health of our brain's storage capacities (Medina, 2008). As students, researchers, and data presenters, we do not have complete control over those aspects for each of our audience members, but we can own our part in this recall process. Effective data presentation, where we use graphic visualization to emphasize information, speeds the acquisition of that information and reduces the opportunity for misinterpretation (Johnson, 2010; Stenberg, 2006).

FIGURE 1.18 Effective data presentation is retained in long-term memory

Because it is so important, here is that statement again: when we adopt the principles discussed in this book, we make it faster for our audience to engage with our work and we reduce their errors. These end results are precisely what we want to encourage among those stakeholders listening to or reading our findings.

Even though some elements of this discussion of visual processing theory have been linearized and oversimplified, the time and effort expended on intentional data presentation are justified. With the above research leading the way, we can make clear to our colleagues, and professors, and supervisors, and clearance departments that our energies are not wasted. The end result is increased audience understanding. If we are not working toward that end, why are we engaged in our work in the first place? The true waste of our own effort, our funding sponsorship, and our audience's time and attention occurs when we retreat back to weak status quo communication because the audience will choose to mentally check out (or check their email).

What Do I Need to Develop Effective Data Presentation?

The research-based principles I detail in this book can move us from the weak presentation to the effective. Additionally, they can elevate the effective presentation to the beautiful, useful, and inspiring. I detail necessary tools and ideas you need to achieve these wonderful goals, supported by your required tools of good cheer and an open-minded disposition.

However, it is important that you know what this book does not address: your content. It does not discuss how you write reports, how well you have designed your study, or the strength of your references; I assume you have all of that under control. Instead, it does discuss how your information gets used by your audiences. In *Utilization-Focused Evaluation,* legendary evaluator Michael Quinn Patton pointed out a set of findings produced in 1995 by the Government Accountability Office on what happens to evaluation reports. The GAO examined the dissemination path of several major federally funded program evaluations in their study, *Program Evaluation: Improving the Flow of Information to the Congress*. This study probably does not sound like a nail-biter, but Patton noted that the report's main finding was that evaluation information does not get very far, despite the significant funding poured into evaluations and the high profile of many of the programs under scrutiny. His point was that we can take strides to make evaluation ultimately more useful by engaging stakeholders throughout the process of the study, ensuring the study examines aspects of importance, and delivering the report to decision makers in time for them to use the information as evidence. But let us tack on to this list of utilization strategies the role of effective data presentation. That same GAO report had these details buried inside: "Lack of information does not appear to be the main problem. Rather the problem seems to be that the available information is not organized and communicated effectively." They went on to say "Information did not reach the right people, or it did, but it was in a form that was difficult to digest" (p. 39). So you see, this book is not about the quality of your content; you are the expert in that area. This book is about organizing that content and communicating it in more digestible and effective ways. Here is what you need.

A Disciplinary Positioning

In addition to learning some concepts around visual processing theory, you should also know how this book fits in with its larger field of study. Knowing this is important to your development as an effective data presenter, because it will tell you where to look for new research and opportunities. And this way, you have more tidbits to share at the next cocktail party when people ask you what you are reading. Data presentation sits at the intersection of closely related fields like usability testing, user-interface design, graphic design, journalism, and document design. All of these areas fall under the broad umbrella of information design. Without a doubt, in the years to come, even more information design subdisciplines will evolve into legitimacy. Here, for the purposes of this book, we focus on data presentation, which encompasses both the layout of our written descriptions of data and the graphic displays of them using data visualizations as well as research-based effective practices from other areas under the information design field. Data visualization has already split into two fields: data visualization that is used for analysis, and that which is used for presentation, which is the focus of this book (as of this writing there is a slight resurgence in discussion among thought leaders trying to clarify this divide—see Gelman & Unwin [2012]). I think an illustration will help diagram these relationships, as I see them intersecting around data presentation.

The ideas from the hybrid zone of data presentation apply to many dissemination formats. In fact, each chapter in the remainder of this book introduces effective practices and applies them to a span of dissemination products you normally use—reports, research posters, slideshows, and the like—and each chapter includes a section that overlays those same principles on data displays themselves.

Shouldn't these topics be split into two volumes—one on reports and one on data visualization? Definitely not. In my studies of evaluation reports, I often came across published tomes that grouped all of the graphs and tables into the report's appendices. So even if we

FIGURE 1.19   Stephanie's classification of the fields influencing data presentation, all of which could be referred to as information design

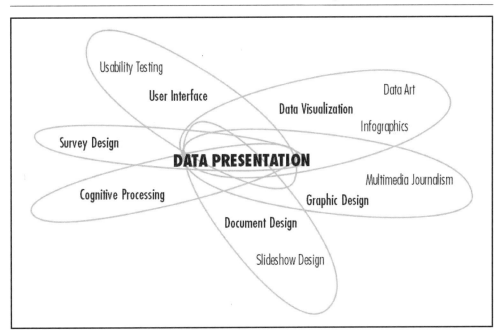

have engaging, inspiring data visualizations, they are not very effective unless we also address reporting as a whole. As I illustrate, the same basic principles apply to the reporting medium and the graphs it contains. Thus, we borrow bits and scraps from many other sources to bear on the work we present in higher education, nonprofits, government offices, and wherever and whatever your location. Information design may not be your main field, but in this process you will become a bit of an interdisciplinarian; that is the 50-cent word to throw around at cocktail parties.

The Software You Will Need

If it is not obvious already, this book is not written for a graphic designer as they would probably find this discussion boring very quickly. If you have a degree in art, you would likely enjoy arguing over the nuances of some of my points (and we can do that, but you have to buy me a coffee first). What you need to know is that this book was developed as a support tool and reference guide for the student scrambling to make a good impression, the social worker engaged in street intervention, the community college faculty member teaching students how to build wind turbines, or the nonprofit executive saving the world with long hours and a tiny budget. People like you. I wrote this book to help my friends and colleagues, who hold down day jobs (which often extend into the night) and just need to know how to kick their presentations up a notch.

That is why all of the examples and demonstrations included in these chapters use software and tools most people already own and can navigate fairly well. You don't have to know any new tools to apply the principles discussed here. I mainly work in Microsoft Office 2010 (and while I wish I was getting some paid product placement for telling you that, instead I am just being honest). In the online companion to the book, Open Office and Google Drive are also included as many people, especially those on very small budgets, are moving to these free platforms. I do not work very often with sophisticated graphic design software, because the learning curve is usually too high and the files are not easily opened by my peers, colleagues, supervisors, and clients. This book illustrates how to use the tools you already own in more effective ways. You probably will not be able to quit your day job to become a professional graphic designer, but you will be able to make a more compelling case out of your work.

The intention is to help you use the tools you already have to make more compelling data presentations so that you can better convince your stakeholders of the worth of your work, secure more attention and funding, and make the world a better place. Please contact me and let me know about your victories after implementing the many suggestions included here.

How Do I Navigate This Book?

The book is designed with icons included throughout the table of contents and chapters so that you can navigate faster when you are whipping up your data presentations on the fly.

FIGURE 1.20 Icons identify places in the book where I discuss reports, slideshows, posters, and graphs, respectively

At any point, tune in to those icons that represent your current task to receive quick refreshers and suggestions. Navigation by way of icons is one method for engaging with this book.

Alternatively, you can explore chapter by chapter. Chapters 2 through 5 represent the four practical groups of graphic design principles that emerged from my research. Chapter 2 starts us out where my research showed we are the weakest—graphics. This chapter discusses how to locate great graphics, how to tell if they are actually great, how to think about the different types of graphics needed for research and evaluation, and what each communicates to the reader. Chapter 3 introduces the main varieties of typefaces and outlines when the use of each variety is appropriate. We specifically review how type can help organize your data presentation and ease engagement for a reader. Chapter 4 is about the proper use of color for legibility, decoration, and spotlighting critical information, including how to locate effective color palettes and then alter the color settings in your software. Chapter 5 illustrates how to arrange the different components (e.g., your text, your photos, your graphs) into a cohesive unit. Details describe how to justify text, how wide columns should be, and even why deleting the legend in your graph increases impact. In Chapter 6, I pull everything together and share some tips on how to make data presentation design more efficient. I also rearticulate the justification that underpins our efforts to communicate effectively. Throughout, the guiding ideas shaping each chapter are applied to reports, slideshows, research posters, and data visualizations. And at the end of each chapter are lists of some of my favorite online resources and activities to help extend your thinking even further.

What Is the Bottom Line?

The three phases of visual processing guide the choices of graphic designers so that their work has a greater likelihood of being encoded in long-term memory. For the rest of us, these skills better clarify our data presentations and support subsequent audience understanding.

The eyes win. People read much faster than they speak. Simultaneous listening and reading, which is common in slideshow presentations, overloads working memory. In the end, this means that the audience did not comprehend the content very well, because their brains are trying to do too many things at once. Presenters often further exacerbate the distractions by adding cartwheeling animation to the slides. This method of presentation actually gets in the way of the audience's attempts to make meaning.

That is not the only place where we get in our own way. As you might have suspected when I was talking about assimilating new information into existing schemas, the more hard-and-fast our existing schemas, the more new information struggles to find a home in long-term memory. Again, I am totally oversimplifying the complexity and nuance of this topic; in addition to the steep learning curve, it is another good reason for us to be wary about the use of visualization tools that can make fancy, artistic diagrams. The research in this area repeatedly shows that when the viewer (young or old) is unfamiliar with the type of display, she spends cognitive energy just trying to understand the display rather than decode the data it is trying to communicate (Chen & Yu, 2000; Shah, Mayer, & Hegarty, 1999). Interpretation slows. Accuracy wanes. The result is that viewers just give up. Super data nerds like me are drawn to curious displays, but in those cases we are more interested in the novelty than the data. Those types of displays tend to showcase the programming expertise of the graph maker in place of supporting audience cognition. Viewers and their brains far prefer simpler displays (Robertson, Fernandez, Fisher, Lee, & Stasko, 2008). This book is not designed to teach you how to make your data look like a sunflower or a cracked windshield; rather it discusses in depth how to make better use of the tools and displays you already know well.

At its core, the techniques in this book can be summarized into two basic strategies: simplification and emphasis. Moving from weak to effective data presentation involves stripping out nonessential information and then adding back in selective emphasis to bring attention to our meaning. In the earlier presentation examples, the weak variety had several things in common. They were cluttered, too full of trivial details, and contained unrelated graphic splash. The effective presentation examples were pared down to the critical information with key graphic elements in place to support the reader's attention.

Presenting data effectively involves taking the strong content you already possess, the software and Internet access you already own, the willingness to be understood and useful (I am confident you have that, too), and the adoption of the accessible strategies contained in the rest of these pages. However, I want to give you a fair warning. What this book shows you, you can't unsee—begin thinking about presentations in this way, and you cannot go back. There is still the option of returning this book to its shelf right now. But this is your last chance. After this, you will always notice weak presentation and know how to make it better. Are you prepared for that inevitable outcome? Are you ready? Me, too.

KEY POINTS TO REMEMBER

The desire is not just to look good. Looking good is the natural outcome of communicating data in line with the way people think about and retain information.

- Information uptake occurs in three phases: early attention, working memory, and long-term memory.

- Graphic design elements and techniques draw attention, help a viewer digest information, and boost the recall of that information later on.

- Effective data presentation uses design principles built around graphics, typeface, color, and arrangement to support engagement with our research products.

HOW CAN I EXTEND THIS?

The exercises below provide websites and activities that can reinforce the concepts presented in this chapter. Do keep in mind that the Internet sources listed can change at a moment's notice. If the URL provided here is not functional, try searching on the keywords to find related material or the website's new location.

Check Out

The International Institute on Information Design at http://www.iiid.net has helpful and authoritative definitions for the bevy of jargon floating around and tons of free user-friendly white papers and books. Download for offline geek-out sessions. Also, take a peek at their list of skills and competencies needed for information designers. You'll be surprised at how you probably already possess these qualities.

The debate around what is data art and what is useful for communication began with this blog post by Nathan Yau, from the FlowingData blog (http://flowingdata.com/2008/12/19/5-

best-data-visualization-projects-of-the-year). Andrew Gelman, more of a statistician, disagreed with Yau's picks, saying they were not functional for many and were too artistic in their display. Several years later, the discussion is still alive, with Gelman and Unwin's (2012) paper on the difference between what they call information visualization and statistical graphs. It is healthy and normal to debate such ideas when a field is under rapid development. Read up on both sides to help you figure out where you stand.

Stephen Few's thoughtful distinction between data visualization and data art (http://www .perceptualedge.com/blog/?p=1245) is also a must read. His point is that data visualization's purpose is to communicate. While I often daydream about making a 6-foot column chart out of clay, our goal in visualizing data should be to support the audience's attention to make meaning from our work. Thus, the types of data displays in this book are not art.

Chris Lysy's cartoons http://freshspectrum.com/—Chris is an evaluation researcher at Westat, and his cartoons are about evaluation, engaging stakeholders, presenting data, and more. His material is hand-drawn from his iPad and they encapsulate the organic, familiar feel that illustrations of that type tend to communicate.

Try This

A sincere thank you to the anonymous person who sent me a preview copy of Don Moyer's *Napkin Sketch Workbook*. In it, he depicts the importance of working with our strong visual literacy skills and walks the reader through how to make simple hand-drawn sketches. The series of sketches throughout this chapter is inspired by Moyer's lessons. Try this example from his book: illustrate the organizational structure of your department and use little stick figures as necessary. Then use circles or some other technique to demarcate the people clustered in various working groups or miniprojects. Look at how the illustration is much more concise (despite how messy you might believe it to be) than the narrative text it would take to explain that diagram and the mental processing energy required to understand such a paragraph.

Similar to the cola experiment I conducted in fourth grade, you can test the dominance of vision among a group of colleagues or classmates using a classic test known as the *Stroop effect*. In this test, read off the words you see on the screen. The words list the names of different colors, except that the words are cast in a color that is different from the word. Go to http://faculty.washington.edu/chudler/words.html to take the Stroop effect test or print out the cards to test and time others. It is harder than you think!

WHERE CAN I GO FOR MORE INFORMATION?

Baddeley, A. (1992). Working memory: The interface between memory and cognition. *Journal of Cognitive Neuroscience, 4*(3), 281–288.

Callaghan, T. C. (1989). Interference and dominance in texture segregation: Hue, geometric form, and line orientation. *Perception & Psychophysics, 46*(4), 299–311.

Chen, C., & Yu, Y. (2000). Empirical studies of information visualization: A meta-analysis. *International Journal of Human-Computer Studies, 53,* 851–866.

Cowan, N. (2000). The magical number 4 in short-term memory: A reconsideration of mental storage capacity. *Behavioral and Brain Sciences, 24,* 87–185.

Gelman, A., & Unwin, A. (2012). Infovis and statistical graphics: Different goals, different looks. Retrieved December 2, 2012, from http://www.stat.columbia.edu/ ~ gelman/research/published/vis14.pdf

Government Accountability Office. (1995). *Program evaluation: Improving the flow of information to the Congress.* PEMD-95–1. Washington, DC: Author. Retrieved October 11, 2010, from http://www.access.gpo.gov/cgi-bin/getdoc.cgi?dbname=gao&docid=f:pe95001.txt

Johnson, J. (2010). *Designing with the mind in mind: Simple guide to understanding user interface design rules.* Burlington, MA: Morgan Kaufmann.

Mayer, R. E. (1997). Multimedia learning: Are we asking the right questions? *Educational Psychologist, 32*(1), 1–19.

Medina, J. (2008). *Brain rules.* Seattle, WA: Pear Press.

Patton, M. Q. (2008). *Utilization-focused evaluation* (4th ed.). Thousand Oaks, CA: Sage.

Robertson, G., Fernandez, R., Fisher, D., Lee, B., & Stasko, J. (2008). Effectiveness of animation in trend visualization. *Transactions on Visualization and Computer Graphics, 14,* pp. 1325–1332.

Shah, P., Mayer, R. E., & Hegarty, M. (1999). Graphs as aids to knowledge construction: Signaling techniques for guiding the process of graph comprehension. *Journal of Educational Psychology, 91*(4), 690–702.

Stenberg, G. (2006). Conceptual and perceptual factors in the picture superiority effect. *European Journal of Cognitive Psychology, 18,* 813–847.

U.S. Dept. of Health and Human Services. (2006). *The research-based web design & usability guidelines* (enlarged/expanded edition). Washington, DC: Government Printing Office.

Ware, C. (2008). *Visual thinking for design.* Burlington, MA: Morgan Kaufmann.

Ware, C. (2013). *Information visualization: Perception for design* (3rd ed.). Waltham, MA: Morgan Kaufmann.

Woodman, G. F., Vecera, S. P., & Luck, S. J. (2003). Perceptual organization influences visual working memory. *Psychonomic Bulletin & Review, 10*(1), 80–87.

Xu, Y., & Chun, M. M. (2006). Dissociable neural mechanisms supporting visual short-term memory for objects. *Nature, 440,* 91–95.

CHAPTER 2

Graphics

Learning Objectives

After reading this chapter, you will be able to:

- Locate high-quality graphics for inclusion in your reports, slideshows, and posters
- Identify the proper size for the graphic
- Place a graphic so that it has impact and supports the related text
- Blend a graphic with its background or surrounding elements
- Build a visual theme
- Decide among methods to increase efficiency of graphic production
- Develop different types of icons quickly
- Handle large file sizes
- Simplify data displays

One of the most effective ways to draw attention and emphasize content in your reporting is through the use of imagery. In addition to catching the early-attentive eye, images, when they are used well, are also good at making their way through working memory to get stored for the long term. Let me tell you a little story about the use of imagery.

I was researching the effectiveness of a jail diversion program for a local county government. Like most counties around the United States, they were strapped for cash. The diversion program was a way to relieve jail overcrowding by releasing low-level offenders into the hands of community resources rather than pay for their

Guiding Ideas

Pictures/graphics are present

Graphics direct toward text

Visual theme is evident

Size corresponds to changes in meaning

Graphics are simple

Graphics are near associated text

extended jail stays. To enter the program, offenders were screened by program staff and asked serious and sensitive questions about drug use history, sexual abuse history, income, and so on. These interviews took place in one room with three other staff, all of whom could be screening other potential participants at the same time, in a space that was about 6 feet by 15 feet, which is smaller than the smallest campus office I have ever seen, with more people inside. And the room had to hold their computers and the files on everyone they had ever screened. You can probably see what I wanted to tell the program funders in our dissemination meeting. Here is an example of a common slideshow used at those types of meetings.

FIGURE 2.1   Typical slideshow with too much text, difficult to read on a textured background

And if I was a common presenter, I would stand at the front of the room reading off the bullet points one by one. The problem with slides of this type again comes back to how our brains receive and react to data. Rates vary, but normal reading speed is two to three times faster than normal speaking speed. In other words, the audience can finish reading the entire list while I am still explaining Bullet 2, but their comprehension is impaired because their brains are trying to do too many things at once. The brain actually does a better job of retaining visual information when it is also paired with verbal information. In fact, a good pairing of these two elements increases retention to 75% (Mayer, 1997). But in this setting where the visual information is all text—the same as is spoken—something is slipping out of working memory.

So, as I told the county commissioners about the situation inside their diversion screening room, I showed them the slide shown in Figure 2.2.

They erupted into laughter. Shortly thereafter, they commissioned a study of the jail to find ways to better utilize their current space (at a time when spending money was a rare activity for county governments); they hired me on for further work, and they chuckled about this slide long after our dissemination meeting was over.

FIGURE 2.2   Clearer slide with fewer words and impactful image

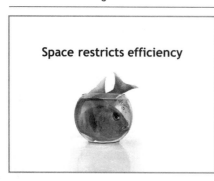

The use of the image highlighted my message. Images stick with people when words do not.

And this reality is also true for presentations, brochures, even technical reports. Whatever method you are using to talk about your research, people tend to only read in-depth if something has caught their eye. As one designer said to me, we live in a "high concept" society; we have about 3 seconds to capture attention, which is hardly enough time to read text. So use an image to help.

How Do I Use Images in Effective Ways?

The presence of graphic elements with associated text results in greater information recall and retention. When used well in data presentations, graphic elements actually help the reader more effectively comprehend our words and our data. There are five ways to use images for effective impact. Images should be:

1. present (seems obvious, but it isn't)
2. emotional
3. placed for high impact
4. quick at communicating
5. repeated

Images Are Present

Imagery tends to be the weakest area of research reporting (Evergreen, 2011). In my dissertation study, the examined research reports contained sparse use of images, and some reports contained no images at all, not even graphs. Therefore, simply the use of images is the first way to be effective at data presentation.

Imagery does not necessarily mean photographs. Graphics can also include charts and diagrams, arrows and other attentional cues, and even lines or blocks of color. The style manual for the American Psychological Association (2010, called APA Guide from here on) refers to *figures* as the umbrella term rather than *graphics,* and includes anything discussed here except tables. Either way, inclusion of these elements leads to greater credibility and increases audience willingness to engage with the material. Graphics and visual imagery are helpful—better than words alone—at making it through the precarious memory path to stick in long-term memory, right where we want our data to go.

Guiding Idea

Pictures/graphics are present

As we discussed in Chapter 1, our working memory is prone to cognitive overload and getting past that hindrance is the tricky part of teaching and presentation. To reduce the risk of overload, a researcher can predigest some of the information. Think of the way a graph represents some mental processing that would have had to take place in the viewer's brain if she was simply reading the information as gray text. Since working memory can only hold roughly four chunks of information at one time, the designer "prechunks," essentially allowing more, richer information into working memory than is otherwise possible.

Pairing an image with a few keywords on a slideshow, or with a few summary sentences in a report or research poster, serves to create a chunk of information mentally processed as one unit. Presenting the combined image-idea pair together replaces lengthy narrative, speeds up the pace at which people engage with our work, and generates more interest in the work. Visuals are powerful presentation tools for researchers.

Images Are Emotional

Imagery is emotional when the viewer feels she can relate. Sometimes this is achieved through empathy, for example when international development organizations depict their under-resourced beneficiaries in their donor appeal letters. But if the goal is to draw an emotional response, the imagery does not always have to be sad or based in power relationships. Emotional imagery can induce pride, the way a university includes images of students at a football game in their promotional materials. With discretion and moderate use, good graphics can evoke delight by being humorous or novel. Emotion can even be stirred by using visual metaphors for a topic, if it is more abstract in nature. The metaphor makes the content more relevant, which is a powerful and compelling emotion. Through the effective use of graphics, readers feel a sense of familiarity and connection (we discuss later in this chapter how that idea applies to graphs). Here is an example of emotive graphic use inserted into a proposal.

I wanted to evaluate a program focused on girl empowerment, so I needed to construct a proposal of my ideas. To make my cover page, I searched through istockphoto.com on the word "empowerment" and found one great, relevant, stock photo.

I believed that this photo would really connect to the client in an emotional way, because these girls are exemplifying the sisterhood and confidence that the program hoped to produce as well. At the time, I think this photo cost about $5 USD. To make it fit on a piece of paper, I combined it with a black box so it would take up the whole page and added text boxes with the title and contact information. This is the completed cover page of the proposal.

FIGURE 2.3   Photograph of girls, arms uplifted, from stock photo website

FIGURE 2.4   Front cover of evaluation proposal using stock photo

After the project commenced, I repeated the same image in the background of my logic model, on the cover of the final report, and in the opening and closing slides of my presentations.

Note that I did not say I pasted the picture on every slide or every page of the report, because that would oversaturate my audience probably to the point where they lose their

FIGURES 2.5 and 2.6   Logic model and front cover of report, both using same stock photo

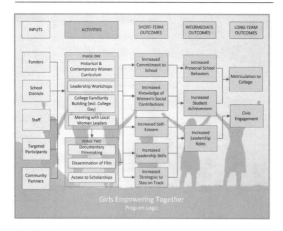

ability to even notice the picture. However, using the image for the introduction and conclusion helped create a brand for me and this particular project. Additionally, all of the evaluation work was now easily recognizable to the client who could quickly distinguish the evaluation materials amongst the multiple piles and folders on her desk (similar to the best professors' offices). I achieved brand recognition, which made me and my work more memorable, and in a very quick and visual way, it helped me keep track of my many projects as well. Nevertheless, more than just the presence of the image, it is the emotion evoked with this particular image choice that makes it work so well.

The emotional response summoned by imagery is weakened when hackneyed pictures are used. A current trend at the time of this writing is the use of faceless, bare, alien-like creatures holding various objects, such as a target or a pencil. These alien figures lack emotion and relevancy and should be avoided. Likewise, the handshake image is so overused that it is glossed over, as is the image of people of various ethnicities holding hands while standing around a picture of the Earth. These images are tired and clichéd, so try to push your thinking a little further.

Images Have Impactful Placement

Graphics and images are effective at catching the eye, right? So, why does their placement matter? The visual impact of your research products increases if the images are large, well blended with the background, and positioned to support the text. All of these elements can be produced by simple word-processing software.

Large and Bleeding

Figure 2.7 is a recommendation slide from the presentation discussed at the start of this chapter. I was pointing out that program staff needed to do a better job hooking the ex-offenders up with community organizations on their way out of jail so that rehabilitation was more successful.

What makes this slide work so well is that the picture of the paperclip and chains takes up the whole slide. It is very large, which is called a full bleed in graphic design world.

Figure 2.8 is a really poor execution of the same slide.

Do not use clip art; actual photography of real images communicates credibility and legitimacy to the viewer (Samara, 2007), even when those images are manipulated with a program like Photoshop. Hand-drawn images, which I love to use, communicate genuineness, directness, and warmth; whereas clip art communicates amateurism. This example of high-quality digital renderings can also work in some situations.

Figure 2.9 is how the image looked when I purchased it from the stock photo site, but it is not quite making the desired visual impact. I increased the visual impact by expanding the photo so that it consumed the entire slide.

To achieve this effect in Microsoft PowerPoint, click on one of the dots at the corner of the photo, and drag it all the way to the corner of the slide. Of course, the image then looked upside down in this case, so I also rotated the image by clicking on the green circle sticking out of the top center and dragging the whole photo 180 degrees. By rotating the image, the direction flows better—from nearby in the upper left to away in the lower right. By expanding the image to fill the screen (bleeding it), I am tapping into the Gestalt theory of closure (see Graham, 2008 for an overview of Gestalt principles in media design). This principle says that our eyes naturally continue the picture off the edges of the screen and into the real world—a good thing when we are trying to make connections from our findings to our audience's circumstances.

Notice how the effect is not quite the same if we stop short of a full bleed, such as in Figure 2.10, or if the image is squished. That is why it is critical to enlarge the image by using the sizing circles at the corners and to expand it fully to the edge of the slide or page—or even off the edge. If it appears that your picture is changing its aspect ratio, right-click on it and choose the Position function, then lock the aspect ratio.

FIGURE 2.7   Recommendation slide expressing a weak link in the program

Connect with resources

FIGURE 2.8   Slide containing clip art

FIGURE 2.9   Slide with image as originally purchased from stock photo website

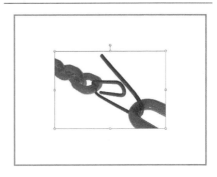

FIGURES 2.10, 2.11, and 2.12 From left to right, slides that are almost bleeding, fully bleeding, and fully bleeding with text

Connect with resources

FIGURE 2.13 Only two of the image's four sides touch the sides of the report page—this is a partial bleed

Sometimes your materials need to contain more words, don't they? And at other times, the picture is just not sized to completely fit a full slide or page, therefore a full bleed picture is not always feasible. Partial bleed is also a good option. In a partial bleed arrangement, the picture takes up a portion of the page, hanging off the edge, while the rest of the page contains words.

Images are easier to manipulate in slideshow software and software like InDesign or Microsoft Publisher that is specifically designed for page layout.

To place an image in Microsoft Word, choose the *Tight* option under the *Wrap Text* tab first. Also under the *Wrap Text* option is the ability to *Edit Wrap Points*. The *Edit Wrap Points* procedure customizes how the words wrap around the image. When this option is selected, it changes the lines around the picture to red, and clicking anywhere along the red lines, lets you create and drag new corners.

FIGURE 2.14 Adjusting the wrap points lets the text flow around the image

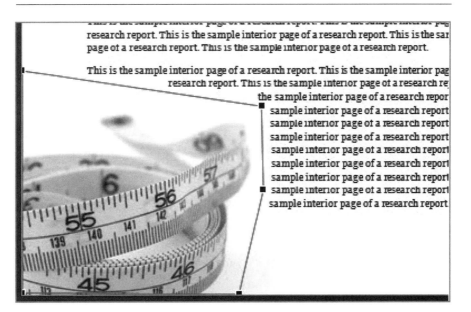

Notice how wrapping points does not work very well in this example because the beginning of each of the first few lines is staggered. This is not visually appealing and can be annoying and difficult for the reader. Wrapping text points works better when the image is on the right.

In this example, the wrap feature still staggers the ends of the lines, but people are used to reading text lines with varying ends (more on that in Chapter 5).

FIGURE 2.15 Moving image and wrapping its points to fit better with the text

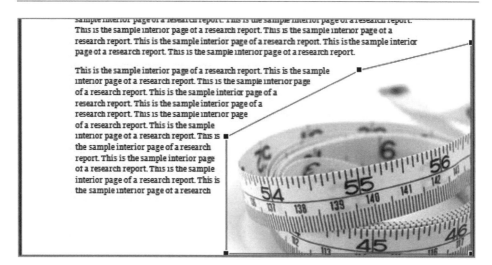

Organizational Logos

It is significant to note that there is one image missing from nearly every case illustration in this chapter—a company logo. In most cases, adding a logo to each slide or on the report cover detracts from the impact of the imagery. At most, departmental or organizational logos are appropriate if they appear in one or two places—perhaps on the inside cover of the report or the thank you slide at the end of a presentation. Think of it this way: If a document is filled with great content and presented in a memorable way, the audience will not forget who you represent.

Matching Background

As you will learn in the chapter on color, the optimal condition for reading is when black or very dark text is placed on a white background. Often the high-quality graphics found in online stock photo sites are isolated on a white background, which makes it easier to match a white page for partial bleed in your document.

Of course, there are situations where you want the background color to be something other than white. Placing a white-isolated picture looks a bit odd. Usually, you can solve this problem by making the picture's background transparent:

FIGURE 2.16 Screenshot of how to set the transparent color in an image

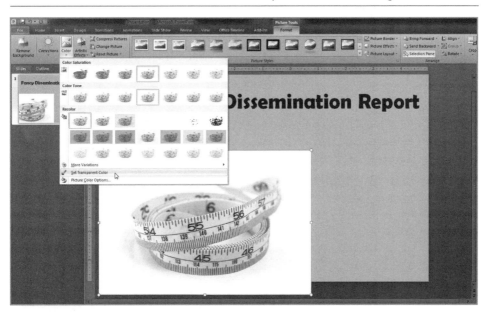

In Word 2010 on a PC, clicking on the picture activates a pink tab called Picture Tools. In the dropdown menu under *Color*, you can select the option *Set Transparent Color*. This option turns the pointer into a pencil. Move the pencil to the white background of the picture and click on it. Every part of the image matching the color where you clicked becomes transparent, which then shows the background color of your document. When using the transparency option, most of the time the end result looks just fine. Sometimes, depending on the quality of the isolation in the picture you purchased, some white still shows.

FIGURE 2.17 Shadows in the stock photo left distracting white areas around the image

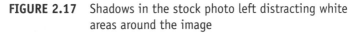

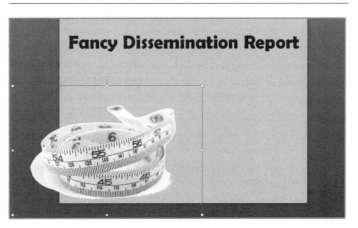

People with access to software like Photoshop or Illustrator can adjust the image so that the white areas no longer appear. It takes time, skill, and access to software that many researchers and graduate students do not have. The simple solution is to use a white background for your document. Another option is to crop down the photo in order to minimize the remaining white areas. If neither of those options work, consider a part-color, part-white background.

FIGURE 2.18   White sections of the slide accommodate stock photos isolated on white backgrounds

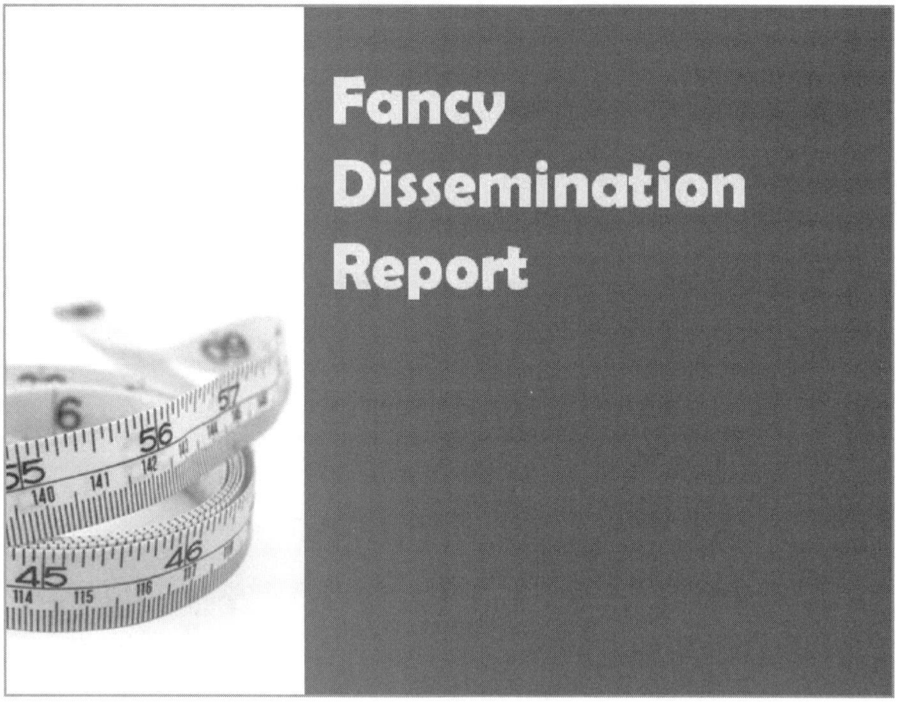

To produce this type of background, I inserted a square, enlarged it to the size of the part of the slide I wanted to cover, and made it gray. Then I put the text box with the words on top of the gray square. Such an arrangement affords minimal image manipulation.

One more option is to shrink the picture and put it in a border. This procedure takes back some of the impact of the full bleed imagery, but it can work in some cases, particularly if people are the subject of the image. However, most of the default borders available in Office or other software packages do not fit for research dissemination purposes, because they can over-manipulate the image. I often use a stock photo of a Polaroid picture frame. I purchased the stock photo once and have used it dozens of times, to frame real photographs of real people.

FIGURE 2.19 Real photograph in poster was positioned inside purchased Polaroid stock photo

I crop down the photograph of the people or enlarge the Polaroid frame to make them fit one another. To layer them appropriately, I click on the people photograph and use the *Send Backward* option.

Guiding Idea

Graphics direct toward text

Facing Text

When working with photos of people, let's talk about the power of eye gaze. Effective use of eye gaze is a powerful way to direct the viewer's eyes toward the text (Reynolds, 2010). For my dissertation study, I reviewed what felt like a billion research reports on human interactions with museum exhibits. Several of the reports integrated actual photos of people engaged with the exhibits, yet in nearly all the selections, the people were positioned with their backs turned to the report's text. Ideally, the report authors should have flipped the photos so that the subjects faced the report narrative. Why does this matter? Humans have a tendency to follow the eye gaze of the subject. In a classroom, if a professor gazes out the window midlecture, the chances are high that the students paying attention also turn their gaze out the window. The same is true with data reports. We want to place the image so that the readers' eyes follow the gaze of the photo subject, toward the text. Compare the impact of the eye gaze and photo placement in these two layouts.

FIGURES 2.20 and 2.21   The better layout positions the eyes of the model toward the text

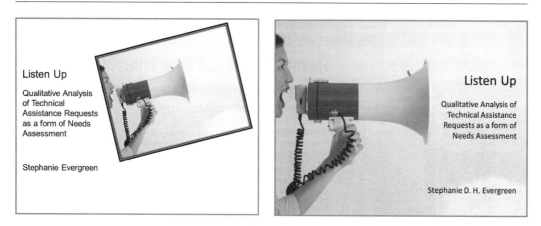

Source: © 2009 Reprinted with permission from EvaluATE.

 The effect is so beautifully subtle that it is barely noticed in Figure 2.21. However, in Figure 2.20 when the eye gaze is not tracking properly, the viewer senses something is wrong. As shown below, the correct eye gaze placement also increases the visual impact of the posters.

FIGURES 2.22 and 2.23   Even if the eyes are not looking directly at the text, it is still a more powerful placement of the graphic

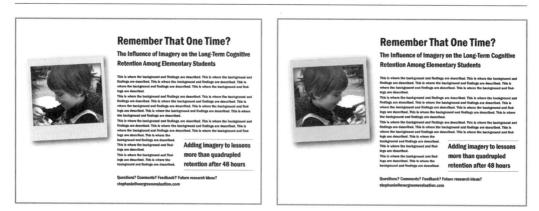

The sense of directionality imposed by the eye gaze works for other nonhuman subjects as well. Everyday objects also have a naturally implied directionality that we can use to guide attention. In turn, that direction dictates the placement of the words. Note the placement of the graphic in this Ad Council advertisement.

FIGURE 2.24   The image of the fish points toward the text

Source: © 2012 Reprinted with permission from the Environmental Protection Agency.

Yes, I suppose there is eye gaze in the image of this fish, but it is really the position of the tail that directs the eyes toward the text. Associatively, it draws some emotion out of the viewer as well. Quite compelling.

Images Quickly Communicate

Graphic elements are useful guides, leading the reader through the organization of a report or slideshow. By identifying and consistently using symbol sets or icons in our documents, we increase the structure of the information, making it easier and quicker for readers to interact with our work. Here are a few types of graphic elements that act as quick visual communication tools.

Reference Icons

Reference icons or symbols are an "easy" way to organize information throughout a report. When I say "easy," what I really mean is their use makes it easier for the reader. Reference icon sets provide the reader with a mental organizational structure, even if they require more work for the report author. It can be difficult to find a set of symbols through stock image sites that adequately conveys the information in the report.

A few sites are listed below where you can procure icons, some of which are free, and some of which come in sets that look like they belong together:

theelearningcoach.com/resources/icon-collection/

www.iconfinder.com/

www.iconarchive.com/

You can quickly see that the number of possible icons can be overwhelming. Just as when searching for good images, it often takes more time than it is worth to find a good match to your reporting needs. So, here is a quick way to make your own icons.

FIGURE 2.25 Reference icons for states included in hypothetical study

I made these state-based reference icons myself in about 5 minutes using Microsoft Word 2010 on a PC.

I started by inserting a text box and typing the two-letter state abbreviations in a cool font (this is Gill Sans Condensed). I made the font size large, in this case 72 points.

FIGURE 2.26 Screenshot of how to change the fill color of text

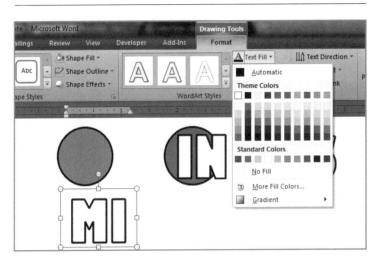

Then (and this exact procedure varies depending on your software program) I used *Text Fill* and selected white and *Text Outline* and selected black. This creates a black outline with white fill. I made the text box itself transparent, or no fill. Easy enough to get the cute outline letters, yes?

For the shape, I just inserted a circle and used the *Shape Fill* and *Shape Outline*:

FIGURE 2.27   Screenshot of how to change the fill color of a shape

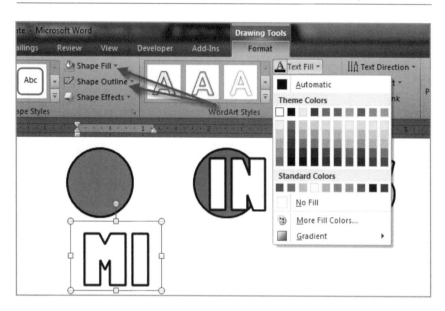

Then I dragged the text box with the letters onto the circle I created and grouped them so that they are easier to move around together. Pay close attention to the placement of each letter set in relation to its circle—you want the letters to appear in pretty much the same spot on each circle. If the letters are centered on one circle and clearly off to the right on another circle, the icons look sloppy. It is okay to use your eyes to judge, but break out the ruler and hold it up to your computer screen if you need to.

FIGURE 2.28   Icon for Michigan

If I want to make it a little more professional, I can add in the state shape behind each abbreviation.

I modified a set of state shapes I downloaded from presentation-magazine.com. The unique shape also helps with quick identification, but it is especially effective to include the abbreviation as well in a case like states (after all, who is able to recognize Wyoming solely by its shape? No offense, Wyomingites).

The similarity in shape and font really give it that feel of an icon set. Now, this set adds impact and structure to my report, which I illustrate in just a few more pages. First, let's examine a few other ways to use reference icons.

In this example, Paul from Community Partners wanted to contrast the classic way organizations operate with the networked way of operating. Here is his original presentation of the concepts.

FIGURES 2.29 and 2.30 Two slides from the deck Paul was originally using

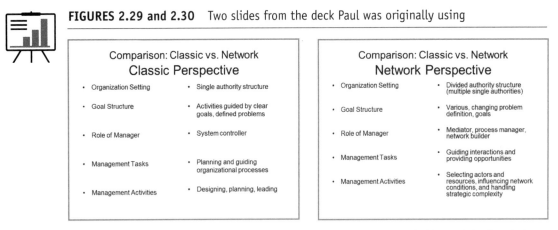

Source: © 2011 *Networks That Work,* http://www.communitypartners.org/. Reprinted with permission from Paul Vandeventer.

Pretty typical, right? I redesigned this talk with Paul to introduce visual depictions of classic and network organizations through the use of reference icons. First, we introduced the two types of organizations.

FIGURE 2.31 Introduction of reference icons for classic and network

Source: © 2011 *Networks That Work,* http://www.communitypartners.org/. Reprinted with permission from Paul Vandeventer.

Then, we repeated the use of those icons when referencing more of their corresponding details. Using reference icons in this manner helps viewers better organize the presented information. Audience members automatically connect one part of the presentation to the next in a visual way.

FIGURES 2.32 and 2.33   Subsequent, explanatory slides with reference icons in corner

Source: © 2011 *Networks That Work,* http://www.communitypartners.org/. Reprinted with permission from Paul Vandeventer.

Judgmental Icons

As current or budding researchers, we are often asked to go beyond our ability to crunch numbers to render our advice or judgment on the topic at hand. Our professional standards in research validity usually encourage us to use very careful wording and defer to the need for future studies on the matter. But often our readers, particularly nonacademic audiences, prefer more straightforward communication. As students we are taught to summarize the main points when we read. Rather than obfuscate that attempt in our own readers, we can use graphics to help us cut to the chase. I like to call these Judgmental Icons (clearly distinct from Emoticons) because they quickly communicate our interpretation of our research findings. You can make up the set that best fits your own work.

Angie Ficek sent me this report to share, where she used judgmental icons to quickly present which aspects of her client's work were most effective. She devised a simple high/medium/low categorization and developed these icons to match.

In her report, of course, she elaborated on the details of each aspect of her client's efforts that worked or did not work, providing the evidence and describing the impact to support her interpretations. Then, she affixed the

FIGURE 2.34   Judgmental icons for high, medium, and low from Angie Ficek

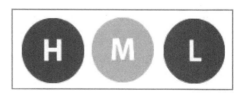

Source: © 2011 Reprinted with permission from the Invitation Health Institute.

appropriate icon to the top of each page so that the bottom line of her research findings was obvious at a glance. She even organized the report in ascending order of effort effectiveness.

FIGURE 2.35 Sample report page with judgmental icon in corner

Peer Influence Programs H

Summary	Peer norms are a strong influence on youth behavior. Some peer influence programs are identified as evidence-based strategies.
Description	Peer influence programs are based on the knowledge that peer norms are one of the strongest factors in youth ATOD use. These programs aim to counter negative peer norms by identifying or recruiting drug-free youth leaders and assisting them to actively serve as role models for same-aged or younger people.
Existing Data	Peer influence programs are very popular and many youth go on to play key roles in their communities' ATOD prevention efforts. Examples of effective peer influence programs include Challenging College Alcohol Abuse, Project Northland, and Lions Quest Skills for Adolescence.
Sustained Impact	Research indicates that peer influence toward ATOD use is one of the strongest correlates with use among youth. The Substance Abuse and Mental Health Services Administration (SAMHSA) has identified the aforementioned programs as evidence-based and included them in their national registry. Such programs have been shown to improve self-efficacy, reduce the number of adolescents using alcohol, and reduce binge drinking in college-aged students.
In Our Community	For more information on the peer influence programs mentioned above, go to www.nrepp.samhsa.gov and search by program name.

4

Source: © 2011 Reprinted with permission from the Invitation Health Institute.

Figure 2.36 has some other options for judgmental icons. For most of these, you can follow the same construction method outlined earlier.

Later, we talk more about color, but avoid using color as the only distinguishing factor between the icons in your set. The stoplight colors (red, yellow, and green in most of the United States) are often used, but they are not such a great idea when used exclusively. They are difficult to distinguish for people with certain types of colorblindness, and they lose their distinction when printed in black and white (and then copied and faxed, as my reports tend to be disseminated after I deliver them to clients). It is perfectly okay to use color, just be certain to also use some other method of differentiation, such as shape.

Images Are Repeated

We gain a visual theme when we use repetition. Repetition occurs when we take a few key graphic elements that support our message and sprinkle them (or variations on them) throughout the document group. For some, the key graphics are the icons we just discussed.

FIGURE 2.36   Just some of the possible sets of judgmental icons

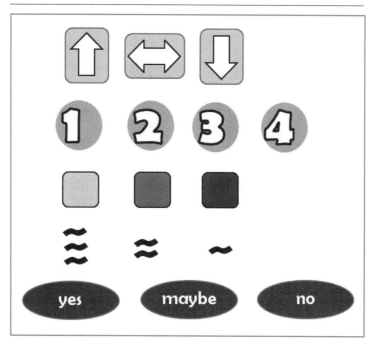

For others, partial bleed images create the visual theme. When we develop a visual theme, we build a system of organization throughout our presentation avenues. Just as with the image of the girls at the start of this chapter, a visual theme works best when it is interwoven in all documents related to the project without being overused. However, it can be repeated in a slideshow where some interior slides feature a cropped-down slice of the original image, as in Figures 2.37 and 2.38.

Guiding Idea

Visual theme is evident

The same image slice can appear on the related handout and on some interior pages of the accompanying report.

Another effective use of graphics to organize a report is to use the interior images judiciously, such as to indicate a change in the report's structure. In Figures 2.39 and 2.40, I show parts of a Greenpeace report on climate change.

Guiding Idea

Size corresponds to changes in meaning

I pulled these images from the middle of the report to highlight how Greenpeace used almost full-page pictures to identify the start of a new report section. Tiny corner images were used to mark that section's interior pages. The size of the image marks meaningful changes to the reader. Such organization speeds up the pace at which readers can navigate with our materials and more readily reveals the author's mental structure for the report.

FIGURES 2.37 and 2.38   Pieces of cover image are repeated on later slides

FIGURES 2.39 and 2.40   Two pages from a Greenpeace report

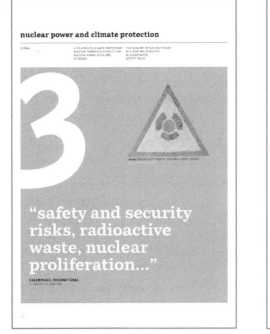

Source: © 2010 Reprinted with permission from One Hemisphere/Greenpeace.

How Do I Efficiently Locate High-Quality Images?

Perhaps the most common remark made by researchers who begin to incorporate graphic images into their work is "But I spend hours just looking through pages and pages of photos. I don't have that sort of time!" No kidding! Let's talk about a few ways to make the job easier: investing in a little conceptual time, using the right stock photo sites, and working with a professional graphic designer.

Invest in Visual Thinking Before Browsing Sites

Perhaps the best way to cut down the time it takes to find high-quality images is to initially spend time, refining what you want. Here is my process: I open PowerPoint and duplicate the initial blank slide so that I have a total of six blank slides. Then I print a page or two so that all six slides fit on one page. It looks like this:

FIGURE 2.41   Print a page of rectangles so you can sketch

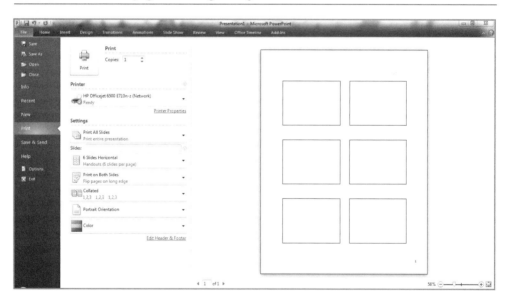

Then I turn off the computer and step away. I sit down with a pencil (and an eraser) and start sketching some ideas. I begin by thinking about the images I tend to associate with the topic at hand. I invest about 20 minutes and engage in some free association, where I basically let my mind wander and my hand doodle, as I test out some visual metaphors. Sometimes, if I am stuck, I grab a colleague to ask what comes to mind when I say the topic name. I might also use a thesaurus or quickly search Google Images to get my juices flowing. The goal during this time is to derive several image possibilities and sketch them into the printed PowerPoint rectangles. Also, I scribble a few words to express the main idea of the slide and maybe a phrase or sentence underneath each rectangle to note what the speaker would be saying at that point. The same process works to develop the template pages for a report: just turn the paper sideways so the rectangles are in portrait orientation and sketch a couple of page layout options.

My sketches are not good—mainly stick figures and lines. But the idea is not to make final artwork, just to get a series of images that ties together to support your main points. For example, let's say I am creating a report for my department chair on a faculty network we have developed. If I simply sit at my computer and search on "network," I get back thousands of images, including topics like computer networks, television networks, and nets. But, by thinking a bit and jotting down some visual ideas before I search, I might conclude that my department chair will be more convinced of the value of the network if I include images that humanize the project. So, I begin sketching images of people interacting, a teacher and a student connecting, a group of happy students.

Then searching sites can be quicker work because you already have a better idea of what to look for. To continue the network example, I can refine my search parameters to include results like people, collaboration, student, teacher, and education. Aside from greater precision in your search terms, also take advantage of the advanced search functions of stock photo sites. Google Images, istockphoto, and other image sites let you add search specifications on file size and even color in the photo. It is a pretty handy way to narrow down the search results in order to spend less time sorting through images. Investing in 15 minutes to gather your visual ideas, and 5 minutes to set up your search parameters, saves an hour or more of digging through the results.

Shop Stock Photo Sites

I am often asked how I found the fishbowl image used at the start of the chapter. I searched "cramped" on istockphoto.com, working with the feelings I experienced when I was in the program office. For the images used in the classic and network organization reference icons, I searched on "hierarchy" and "teamwork," respectively. I typically work with professional stock photo websites and pay a small amount for each photo I use; I build the stock photo price into my project budget.

The generous Internet universe also provides us with several sites that hold free stock photos. Currently, Creative Commons, stockxchg, morguefile, and Google Images are popular options. Google Images can seem like a great idea until you search. I searched on "teamwork" and got about 37,400,000 results. Wow! However, be careful—most of the images you find in a simple Google search are owned by someone else, and it is illegal to just copy and paste them into your own report. Google's search technology is getting better at helping us locate available photos we can use for free. Use the Advanced Search function in Google Images (at the time of this writing I clicked on a little gear icon and then clicked *Advanced*

Search). Then specify the usage rights and elect to only view those images of "teamwork" that are available to use, share, and/or modify for free. When I search again on "teamwork," (with usage rights checked that allow for commercial reuse—the usage required if I wanted to, say, put this in a department brochure), Google returned just 65 images. Thus, there are fewer images to sort, and I can be more confident of copyright law compliance.

Despite the time spent, searching on free photo sites like Google Images and stockxchg can often return options that just do not work. At least on Google, many of the images are personal photos. Some are too casual—they look like they were taken by someone like me (an amateur rather than a real photographer). The lighting is too dark; the photo is too cluttered. Imagine if I took a photo of a Little League baseball team. The photo is probably just a bit too casual and messy—telephone wires cutting in front of the image, too much fence and not enough team, a mom mid-bite on her hot dog. Perhaps that realism is exactly right for your project. It often is—I have read research reports where it definitely makes sense to have real photos, of real people, really interacting. But, for different dissemination settings, you might want a more professional and cleaner image. On paid stock photo sites, the great majority of the images are just that—clean and simple. Often, they are taken in controlled environments with no backgrounds that add clutter or "noise" to your page or poster. The search results are almost always restricted to high-quality images, which reduces the amount of necessary sorting and saves you precious time.

> ## Guiding Idea
> Graphics are simple

Many stock photo sites make the work of locating a relevant, emotional, high-quality image much easier. Except, before you invest in a photo, be certain you are purchasing the size that fits your dissemination. Typically, size is offered in a few different ways. The default is often set in pixels; pick something close to the resolution of the screen where you will be displaying the image. Resolution is different for every computer. On mine, I right-click on my desktop and choose *Properties*. I use two monitors and the Properties window tells me that on Monitor 1, my resolution is 1366×768. Therefore, for full-screen graphics I want pixel dimensions that are very similar.

Projectors use whatever resolution is on your computer, so don't worry about the projection screen being 10 times larger than your laptop screen.

Now, pixel dimensions are for screen display. To also use those images on paper requires more information. Look for details about the dpi. It stands for dots per inch and it's one of the components that leads to fuzzy graphics, which occurs when the dpi is too small and the report designer tries to overenlarge the few dots per inch. If you are using the graphic for paper printing, you need to purchase 300 dpi.

Finally, look at the dimensions in inches. Even if you have the right dpi for your dissemination purpose, if you purchase a photo that is only 3" × 5," it will look blurry and unprofessional if you try to stretch it to fill your report cover page. In that case, purchase something nearer to 8.5" × 11" (for the standard U.S. paper size). A better but pricier option is to search for and purchase vector versions of your favorite images, which are infinitely resizable. Stock photo sites are generally quite easy options for high-quality photos. You need to learn a little bit of decoding to understand the pricing scheme, but doing so can save your project budget some major cash.

Hire a Graphic Designer

An instinct for great design can be learned. If you are reading this book, you are showing sufficient interest in this topic that you can use to develop your own amazing information design skills. When the stakes are high, when the project will produce a great deal of documentation and you will be in front of important audiences, I am confident that the strategies presented throughout this book will enable you to shine. However, despite a high skill level, researchers and students are often a very busy crowd, running from class to meetings to office hours and back again. Those of us in such a position may be better off working with a professional graphic designer who can refine existing products and develop templates for future work.

In one of my projects, we received a large four-year grant in which we promised to produce mountains of printed material, including research resources, newsletters, slideshows, and handouts. Thus, we sat down with a graphic designer in our very early days, spent about 2 hours discussing the types of templates we wanted, the software available in-house, and the image we wanted to project through our logo. For about $5,000 USD, the designer returned a whole branded package that we then used throughout the grant.

Even so, as the client of the graphic designer, it is still important to prepare imagery ideas, color scheme possibilities, and thoughts about your own presenting style so that the graphic designer can be most efficient. The APA Guide recommends sharing the guidelines in its Figures chapter when working with a contracted professional designer. Still, you need to be able to judge whether the design represents your work well and meets your needs. In other words, whether you choose to outsource your design work or build it yourself, the material in this book helps you become a more informed design consumer and a better client.

What If My File Size Becomes Too Large?

Adding high-quality images definitely increases the size of files. For some, this may make it difficult to attach to an email. Here are four ways to deal with large files:

Delete cropped areas of pictures. If you have been working with graphics, you have probably cropped, sliced, and diced some down to the right size. But the cropped areas just stay hidden rather than deleted, keeping the file size large.

To delete the cropped areas, after inserting the first picture, click on the picture so it is activated and then click on the *Picture Tools* menu that appears (in Office 2010 on a PC, this shows up as a pink tab). Navigate over to *Compress Pictures* and click to open the options there.

Be certain that *Delete cropped area of pictures* is checked. Do not check *Apply only to this picture* and that way you only have to enact this procedure once. In this options menu, the quality of the picture can be changed as well, which also adjusts the file size. By following this process, the total file size of my 25-slide PowerPoint file with large pictures on each slide decreased by about one-quarter.

FIGURE 2.42   Screenshot of how to delete cropped areas of pictures

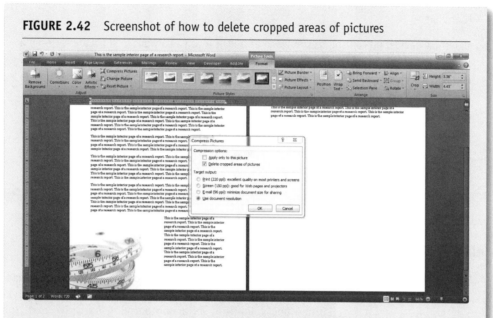

We are not into the font chapter yet, but another option is to unembed fonts. On the same slideshow just mentioned, this process saved me about 10% more space. In Office 2010 on a PC (not available in Office 2008 for Macs), click on *Save As*. Before saving the file, click the arrow just to the left of the Save button and choose *Save Options* from the drop-down menu. This box will open:

Check out the options under *Embed Fonts*. If your document consists only of the most common fonts (Times New Roman, Calibri) you can probably just uncheck the main box for the maximum file size decrease. Other options there also minimize file size. Unembedding fonts can be risky, however, as I demonstrate in the Fonts chapter.

Saving in the PDF format also decreases file size. Often,

FIGURE 2.43   Screenshot of how to unembed fonts

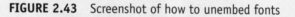

(Continued)

(Continued)

slideshow navigation can still be preserved as a PDF. If you also want to show the Notes in a slideshow, save your show through the printing function. In the printing options, select *Notes Pages* and then print to PDF. PDF is not always ideal, particularly in circumstances where you need to collaborate, but it can work in many situations.

Finally, if none of the previous suggestions are sufficient, use a cloud service to transfer files. Dropbox and other file transfer services are free to use and contain enough space to hold large, image-heavy documents. Simply sharing a link with others allows access to the documents for download.

Where Should Graphs Go?

Guiding Idea

Graphics are near associated text

Finally, let's take care of one of the most common mistakes I see in research reporting. Typically, once the main report narrative starts, it just runs on page after page. As such, a graph is sometimes split from its accompanying narrative text, for example in the image below.

FIGURE 2.44   The bottom of one page, containing narrative, and the top of the following page, with the graph

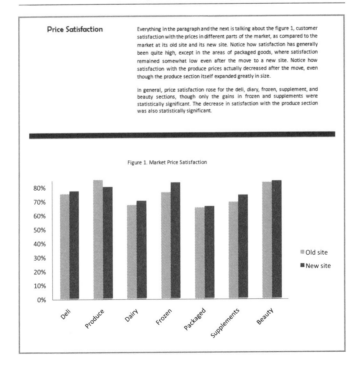

Here we are looking at the bottom of one page, where the narrative is located, and the top of the next, where the reader finds the associated graph. Sometimes, I even see research reports where all of the graphs are grouped in an appendix, pages and pages away from their corresponding text. But, even if the graph is just on the next page, any flipping back and forth between pages to try to cohere the two blocks of information impairs readers' ability to comprehend; we lose them when they have to flip. It is better to isolate one idea per page or at least to start the idea on the page where the graph is located. Just use the *Page Break* option in your word-processing software at the start of a new idea. In Figure 2.45, the narrative and the graph are grouped together, immediately easing comprehension.

FIGURE 2.45 Narrative and graph now coexist on a single page

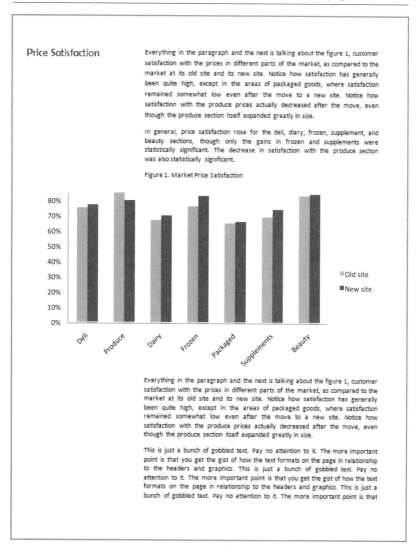

How Do I Apply These Ideas to Graphs?

Naturally, data displays are most effective when they are visualized using the appropriate type of graph. Generally speaking, humans are good at judging length and bad at judging area—which means bar and line charts are often good options. Bar charts work best when comparing categories. Line charts are most appropriate for looking at change over time. Scatterplots most effectively represent correlations and linear relationships.

Choosing Chart Types

Several tools are at our disposal to help choose the appropriate type of chart, thanks to the divine power of the Internet. With each of these tools, the user begins by identifying the relationship between the variables. What is the objective? Are you trying to show change over time or part-to-whole relationships? The program then limits the available chart options to those designed specifically for the targeted relationship, thus taking out the guesswork.

Check out the Chart Chooser at Juice Analytics: labs.juiceanalytics.com/chartchooser/index .html. Tableau has a white paper on the topic, freely available in exchange for your contact information: www.tableausoftware.com/learn/whitepapers/which-chart-or-graph-is-right-for-you.

Once you establish the type of display most appropriate for your data, err on the side of simplicity when designing the display. We cover more on this topic in later chapters, but for now, let's focus on these three attributes:

1. Two-dimensional
2. Free of extraneous lines
3. Familiar to viewers

Guiding Idea

Graphics are simple

Two-Dimensional

Of course, two-dimensional displays are simpler than three-dimensional data displays. Although many graphing software programs supply three-dimensional templates, it does not necessarily assist graph interpretation or accuracy (Few, 2006; Malamed, 2009). Here's an example of a data display, showing customer satisfaction with prices both before and after a health food store moved location. I am providing the table here so that you can see the exact data points.

When using Excel 2010, I select the entire table and ask the software to create a bar chart. The default 3-D version of the chart in Excel is Figure 2.47. I know, I know—the y-axis should always start at 0 and here I have started it at 63%. I am cheating just a little here so that we can take a closer look at the tops of the columns and bars.

In this comparison, notice how it is not obvious where to read the top of the columns to get the exact data point—do we read the back of the column? The front edge? The midpoint of the top of the column? Actually, it is none of these. See the tallest column, representing Produce at the old site? In the table, we can see that data point is supposed to be 85%. Yet no part of the 3-D column

FIGURE 2.46 Table of percentages of respondents satisfied with prices in various grocery sections at old and new store location

Price Satisfaction	Old site	New site
Deli	75%	77%
Produce	85%	80%
Dairy	67%	70%
Frozen	76%	83%
Packaged	65%	66%
Supplements	69%	74%
Beauty	83%	84%

reaches the 85% line. When we simplify the graph to a 2-D model, which is Figure 2.48, the tops of the bars match exactly with the data points in the table.

FIGURES 2.47 and 2.48 Same data, displayed in 3D and 2D

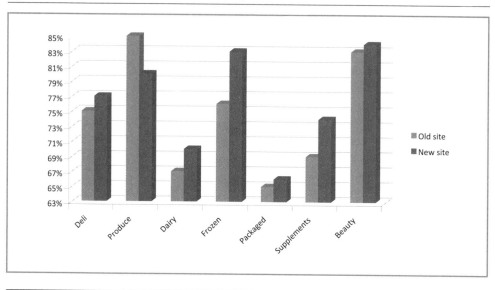

FIGURES 2.47 and 2.48 (Continued)

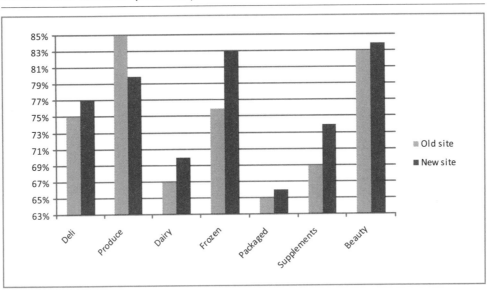

Free of Extraneous Lines

Even the 2-D version of the graph can be simplified in order to more efficiently present the data. We can enhance reader interpretability by turning down what Edward Tufte (2001, p. 105) called the "noise" in the graph. By "noise," I refer to all of the parts of this graph that don't actually display data or assist reader cognition. At this point, let's focus on creating more empty space by removing unnecessary lines. We start with the default chart on the left, this time with an appropriate y-axis.

FIGURES 2.49 and 2.50 Same graph, with and without the gridlines

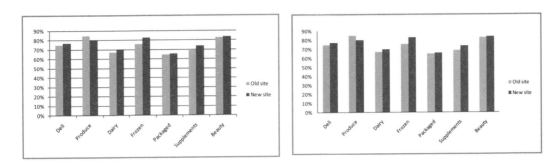

The simplified version of the graph is on the right. First, I removed the chart border. Graphics often appear more integrated with the narrative when we remove the box and let the white spaces just blend. Then I deleted the gridlines, simply by clicking on them and hitting the Delete key. For those of you who really, really like the gridlines, you can alternatively right-click on the gridlines and choose a very faint gray color. The appearance with no gridlines is a cleaner look, but a faint grid is better than the default. I also removed the tick marks on both axes. To do this in Excel 2010, right click on an axis and select *Format Axis* and chose *None* from the dropdown menu for *Tick Marks*. (Note: The APA Guide asks for tick marks, but if the document is not being submitted to an APA journal, you can do without them.) Some bold people might delete the axis line altogether. If you are ready to tackle that, head to Chapter 5. For now, though, we drastically simplified the graph and as a result, it is easier to interpret.

Now that we simplified the graph, we can add back design graphics to cue the viewer's attention and quickly communicate a key message.

FIGURE 2.51 Addition of a simple target line

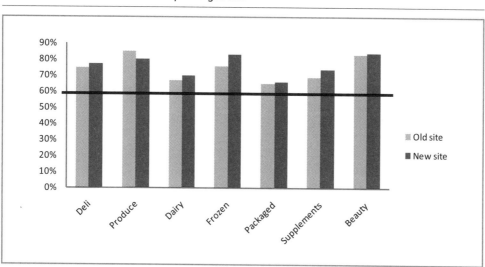

In this version of the graph, I added back a target line to indicate that the store expected at least 60% of customers to be satisfied with prices in each area.

Now apply some of the guiding ideas we learned in this book so far to the graphs. Introduce those cute state icons from earlier. In this example, I am trying to compare key indicators (rates of graduation, obesity, and home ownership) between Michigan; our nemesis to the south, Indiana; and the national average. (All numbers are totally fictitious.)

Below, I show how a typical table looks and then illustrate how the addition of the reference icons begins to give it more visual interest.

FIGURES 2.52 and 2.53 Same table, with and without reference icons

	Michigan	Indiana	National
Graduation	76.3	74.1	74.9
Obesity	30.5	29.1	33.8
Home Ownership	73.1	71.7	67.4

	MI	IN	US
Graduation	76.3	74.1	74.9
Obesity	30.5	29.1	33.8
Home Ownership	73.1	71.7	67.4

Obviously, I know it does not do much to add icons to one table. However, when we use the icon system in each data display throughout the report, we build a predictable organizational structure that speeds recognition and aids comprehension.

FIGURES 2.54 and 2.55 Data displays that capitalize on the introduction of reference icons

These figures look even better when a color system is added. Check out these examples at our website (www.sagepub.com/evergreen) to see what the full color plus reference icon system can look like.

Familiar to Viewers

You are not limited to representing your data only in bar or line graphs. The world of data visualization is full of awesome new developments in the ability to display data on maps or trees. I encourage the exploration of those new tools, some of which, like Tableau, have free versions. Just try to avoid some of the pitfalls when trying out new types of graphing.

A common mistake that impedes comprehension is when size changes in the graph do not actually correspond to meaningful changes in the data. I reproduced here what I have seen several times in research reports, which was intended to show the response percentages for a Likert-type scale. But, in many

Guiding Idea

Size corresponds to changes in meaning

of the versions I saw (see example below), the sizes of the circles do not accurately or proportionately represent that data. The circle representing Agree is not really 61 times the size of the circle representing Strongly Disagree.

FIGURE 2.56 Typical bubble graph that is difficult to accurately interpret

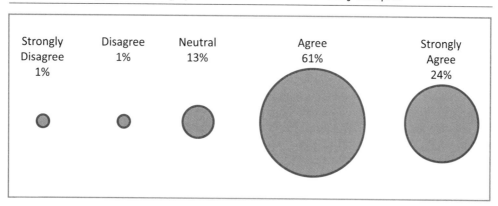

There is some debate in the data visualization field as to whether circles should be sized by their area or diameter. And if the graph designers are still trying to figure out the best way to display circles then imagine the confusion for an average viewer. The use of circles is particularly challenging—another reason to stick to simple bar and line graphs.

In ideal circumstances, a reader should be able to apply a ruler directly to the lengths of bars and calculate ratios that are equivalent to the ratios of the data that are represented by the bars. Space often limits our ability to properly size charts, such as in the case of this book. However, at the least, we can follow the recommendations from the APA Guide, which suggest that graphics of equal importance be equally sized in a report.

As pretty as they might be, please be a bit cautious about getting caught up in sophisticated software and using complicated data displays. Maps, of course, are familiar to most readers. Nevertheless, other types of data displays can look more like a demonstration of the extent of the tool's awesomeness or researcher's prowess rather than a way to support reader cognition.

Research has repeatedly shown that simpler visualizations are interpreted more efficiently and lead to better recall (Tractinsky, 1997). Clean, simple, beautiful visualizations keep viewers interested and engaged for longer periods of time; whereas viewers are more likely to skip visualizations that are cluttered, confusing, or elaborate (yet there is still some debate—see the study by Bateman, Mandryk, Gutwin, Genest, McDine, & Brooks [2010] that suggests strong imagery around standard graph types can improve memorability via the pictorial superiority effect). Generally, the more familiar the basic structure of the graph, the greater your audience's ability to engage.

What Is the Bottom Line?

For many of us involved in research, we are accustomed to descriptive, academic report writing. We explain. Metaphors, especially visual ones, rarely had a place in our data presentation, to the detriment of our audience. Thus, this is your license to allow room for creative thinking. For effective presentation, you need to succinctly name your key messages and identify visual images or metaphors that extend and elaborate on them. I know a few situations where the researcher handed off the development of visuals to a research assistant or the departmental receptionist. In almost all cases, these did not work out well. It is not that a research assistant or secretary lacks the skill to create nice graphics—everyone can achieve that skill if needed. It is just that the development of good visuals takes a more intimate knowledge of the data, the main findings, and the key message the audience should take away. I know and appreciate that everything I discuss in this chapter requires you to invest your time, and maybe even a bit of your money, and you are busy. But the payoff is huge—it is increased audience engagement, interpretation, and understanding.

KEY POINTS TO REMEMBER

High-quality graphics increase the impact of your data presentations.

- High-quality graphics have minimal clutter. In terms of photographs, stock photo sites are one solid option for finding controlled graphics. In terms of data displays, nonessential gridlines, axis labels, and tick marks can be removed.

- Whether free or for a fee, images should be procured at the right size so they are crisp when presented. Check pixel resolution, dpi, and size.

- Simplified graphics can be altered to draw attention to key areas through the use of selective emphasis techniques.

- A strong visual theme is built when graphic elements, such as portions of the same picture, or the same color, or the same shapes, are repeated throughout the data presentation suite.

HOW CAN I EXTEND THIS?

Check Out

Presentation Magazine (http://www.presentationmagazine.com/editable-maps)—This site is filled with free downloadable material and it is where I accessed the editable map files I talked about earlier. Do not use the download directly, because it is recognizable as a template: instead modify it to make it your own.

Creative Commons (http://search.creativecommons.org/)—Creative Commons licenses release images for public consumption and come in a variety of styles, some of which allow for commercial use and modification of the original image. Searching for images in the Creative Commons is a good way to narrow your results to those that are reusable. Be certain to become familiar with the various license categories.

Slideshare (http://www.slideshare.net/)—Browse around on this site for imagery inspiration. Type your subject area into the search field and explore the results. Much of the material posted here is aligned with the guiding ideas presented in this book. Consider uploading your own awesome slideshow to inspire others.

Try This

Get into small groups of three to four people. Take turns sharing your topic (in a word or two) and letting the others brainstorm synonyms or visual metaphors using free association. Jot down all of the ideas (try not to dismiss anything at this point) in a list and then move on to the next activity suggested here.

Print out or draw a six-up page of blank slides and sketch visual imagery representing the synonyms or metaphors you just brainstormed.

Review your last report or paper and identify at least two places where a stronger visual metaphor would help support your point.

Find a research report online in your disciplinary area and identify where graphics could be added or taken away. Graphics are dramatic and attract attention, so they should be used judiciously. Graphing the responses to every survey question, for example, dilutes the impact. Reserve graphics for your most important points.

WHERE CAN I GO FOR MORE INFORMATION?

American Psychological Association. (2010). *Publication manual of the American Psychological Association* (6th ed.). Washington DC: Author.

Bateman, S., Mandryk, R., Gutwin, C., Genest, A., McDine, D., & Brooks, C. (2010). Useful junk? The effects of visual embellishment on comprehension and memorability of charts. *ACM Conference on Human Factors in Computing Systems* (CHI), Atlanta, GA, pp. 2573–2582.

Evergreen, S. D. H. (2011). *Death by boredom: The role of visual processing theory in written evaluation communication.* (Unpublished doctoral dissertation). Western Michigan University, Kalamazoo, MI.

Few, S. (2006). *Visual communication: Core design principles for displaying quantitative information.* Retrieved September 9, 2010, from http://www.perceptualedge.com/articles/Whitepapers/Visual_Communication.pdf

Graham, L. (2008). Gestalt theory in interactive media design. *Journal of Humanities & Social Sciences, 2*(1), 1–12.

Jamet, E., Garota, M. & Quaireau, C. (2008). Attention guiding in multimedia learning. *Learning and Instruction, 18,* 135–145.

Lusk, E. J., & Kersnick, M. (1979). The effect of cognitive style and report format on task performance: The misdesign consequences. *Management Science, 25*(8), 787–798.

Malamed, C. (2009). *Visual language for designers: Principles for creating graphics that people understand.* Beverly, MA: Rockport.

Mayer, R. E. (1997). Multimedia learning: Are we asking the right questions? *Educational Psychologist, 32*(1), 1–19.

Reynolds, G. (2010). *Presentation Zen design: Simple design principles and techniques to enhance your presentations.* Berkeley, CA: New Riders.

Robins, D., Holmes, J., & Stansbury, M. (2010). Consumer health information on the web: The relationship of visual design and perceptions of credibility. *Journal of the American Society for Information Science and Technology, 61*(1), 13–29.

Samara, T. (2007). *Design elements: A graphic style manual.* Beverly, MA: Rockport.

Tractinsky, N. (1997). Aesthetics and apparent usability: Empirically assessing cultural and methodological issues. Paper presented at the *CHI 97 Conference Proceedings.* New York: ACM, 115–122.

Tufte, E. R. (2001). *The visual display of quantitative information* (2nd ed.). Chesire, CT: Graphics Press.

CHAPTER 3

Type

Learning Objectives

After reading this chapter you will be able to:

- Distinguish between different categories of fonts
- Identify the proper application of those different categories
- Appreciate font "personalities"
- Make informed choices about type size
- Calculate appropriate line spacing
- Protect font choices
- Mark levels of importance with type
- Organize type in a data display

As I finalize an evaluation of a report for work, my usual process is probably similar to yours. I spend an afternoon fussing with the layout and putting the polish on a report before sending it off to my boss for one last review. I did just that with a report page similar to the one I am showing you here.

I am using this page (see Figure 3.1) as my example because it is probably where I spent the most time. It was important to me (and now I am really letting on how far I am willing to go) that this table contained rows of equal height. This required some nudging, squishing, and testing until the table was just right. Then I emailed it to my boss and asked him to give it a last inspection before I shipped it out to the client.

Instead of sending it back to me, he saved me a step and passed the report directly to our clients. I am an easy-going person. I was not bothered by his actions, but I did want an approved and finalized copy of the report for my own records, so I opened up his attachment and a version similar to Figure 3.2 was what I saw.

Guiding Ideas

Text fonts are used for narrative text

Long reading is in 9- to 11-point size

Body text has stylistic uniformity

Line spacing is 11 to 13 points

Headings and callouts are emphasized

No more than three fonts are used

Bullets are slightly less thick than text

At that point, I freaked out. Now, if you aren't a bit of a nerd about these things, which I admit I am, you may not immediately notice the differences between these two versions of the report. First of all, the perfectly spaced table was ruined in that one of the rows grew in height when a word in the first column (Islander) jumped down to a third line. Second, the heading and narrative fonts both look different. And, to add insult to injury, the last paragraph on my original page walked the plank in the version on the right.

Our report was struck by a very annoying phenomenon called font substitution. I am sure it has happened to you, too. You email your poster to your copresenter and when she receives it, the formatting is wacky. You plug your flash drive into the conference session room laptop only to discover it does not look at all how you intended. By the end of this chapter, you will have several strategies on hand to ensure that you are not plagued by these same issues.

FIGURE 3.1 A painstakingly formatted report page

Appendix

The table below shows demographic composition over the duration of the initiative. Ultimately the changes show that the initiative's primary target population has grown older, more female, and more racially diverse.

Race (by percent)

	2010-11	2011-12	2012-13	Overall Change (in percentage points)
American Indian or Alaska Native	2	4	2	0
Asian	8	10	9	+1
Black or African American	12	13	14	+2
Hispanic/Latino	8	6	11	+3
Middle Eastern	0	2	4	+4
Multiracial	5	7	10	+5
Native Hawaiian or Other Pacific Islander	0	0	0	0
White	65	58	50	-15

As you can see from the table, the initiative has yet to attract any Native Hawaiian or Other Pacific Islanders, despite their representation in the larger organization population.

As we stated in the report, while it appears that the initiative attracted and then lost some who were American Indian or Alaska Native, in reality those participants were a part of one division that was purchased by another organization in late 2012.

Finally, while it may appear from the percentages that the white population decreased, their raw numbers were steady while participation increased from other racial groups.

FIGURE 3.2   How the report page looked to the recipient

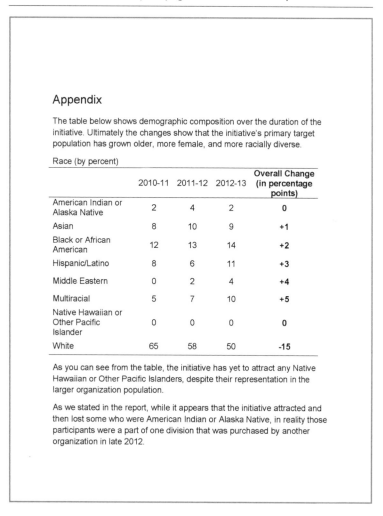

Appendix

The table below shows demographic composition over the duration of the initiative. Ultimately the changes show that the initiative's primary target population has grown older, more female, and more racially diverse.

Race (by percent)

	2010-11	2011-12	2012-13	Overall Change (in percentage points)
American Indian or Alaska Native	2	4	2	0
Asian	8	10	9	+1
Black or African American	12	13	14	+2
Hispanic/Latino	8	6	11	+3
Middle Eastern	0	2	4	+4
Multiracial	5	7	10	+5
Native Hawaiian or Other Pacific Islander	0	0	0	0
White	65	58	50	-15

As you can see from the table, the initiative has yet to attract any Native Hawaiian or Other Pacific Islanders, despite their representation in the larger organization population.

As we stated in the report, while it appears that the initiative attracted and then lost some who were American Indian or Alaska Native, in reality those participants were a part of one division that was purchased by another organization in late 2012.

What Is Type?

Type refers to the shapes of the individual letters and to the stylistic variations that contribute to legibility in different contexts. I love to think about how there is a type designer sitting in a foundry somewhere in the world, crafting a new lowercase letter *t* to improve on the 13 *t's* I already used in this sentence. For most of us, at first glance the differences in the angle of the curvature at the top of a *t* do not seem like a big deal. Yet we happily and usually unknowingly are on the receiving end of such careful thought all around us, every day. We do not need to worry ourselves too much with the specifics of creating letter shapes. We just need to know how to use them well in order to present data effectively.

Most of us refer to this topic area using the word "font." I do. During my dissertation study, when I developed the four main topic areas that are now sections of this book, the graphic designers on my review panel disagreed. The conversation went like this:

Me: "So, I'll break out these principles into Graphics, Color, Font, and Arrangement."

Peter: "You can't call it font. It's called typeface."

Me: "Typeface? Who says that? Everybody I know calls it font."

Peter: "Fine, well, then just call it type. This is very different from font."

Me: "Call it type?! Don't you know that in the real world there are lots of different meanings for the word type? I'm calling it font."

Peter: "Font is what you see. Typeface is what you design with."

Me: "..."

If you relate Peter's comments to your graphic design friends, they will think you are very effective. However, for the rest of us and throughout this book, I use font, type, and typeface pretty interchangeably. Don't tell Peter.

How Do I Tell These Typefaces Apart?

There are two basic types, or categories, of type.

Serif

FIGURE 3.3   Serif fonts are one of the major font categories (from top to bottom: Baskerville Old Face, Georgia, Times New Roman)

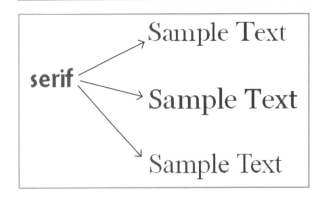

The first class of fonts is serif. The top option in Figure 3.3 is Baskerville Old Face. Now, this may sound silly, but font nerds like me enjoy a feisty discussion about how fonts have personalities. For example, the properties of Baskerville Old Face are said to reflect a more professional, serious, focused, yet comfortable personality.

The next serif down the line is Georgia. Georgia's personality is known as friendly and intimate. Do you see those personality traits when you compare Georgia to Baskerville Old Face? Georgia is an effective choice for tiny print because it is highly legible, even at small sizes.

The third serif example shown is Times New Roman. Times New Roman has a reputation. It is seen as sturdy and classic. But it is a bit of a flashpoint for type nerds. Times New Roman is commonly used in newspapers because it is so easily read at a small size. It also was the default typeface in Microsoft Word. For those reasons, some say it is overused, past its prime, and even a little cold.

So while these are all a bit different, what they have in common is that they are serif fonts.

Guiding Idea

Text fonts are used for narrative text

Serif is a Latin word that means "little feet." See the little feet at the bottom of the letters? Those feet help create an almost continual line along the bottom of a length of text, smoothing the reading process. Serif typefaces make reading our work more fluid (Song & Schwartz, 2008). Research consistently shows that fonts with a serif are easier to read, especially in lengthy smaller print. The APA Guide (2010) says serif fonts are preferred. The MLA guide (2009) wants something "easily readable" (p. 116) and suggests Times New Roman.

FIGURE 3.4 All serif fonts have little feet at the ends of the lines that make up each letter

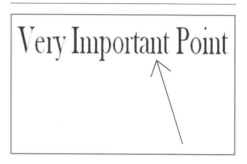

You should probably pick a serif font for at least the body text of a written report where we expect an audience to engage in sustained reading. In a sidebar here, the guiding idea refers to these as "text fonts" instead of "serif fonts." I promise that I am not intentionally throwing more jargon into the mix. My rationale for this becomes apparent in just a few more pages.

Sans Serif

Titles, headings, and callouts may be a good place to have a little more fun, especially since they are bound to be a larger size and a shorter burst of text. It is perfectly appropriate to choose a sans serif or a "no little feet" font in those places.

Guiding Idea

Headings and callouts are emphasized

FIGURE 3.5   Sans serif fonts are the other major category of type—no little feet here (from top to bottom: Baskerville Old Face, Arial, and Jokerman)

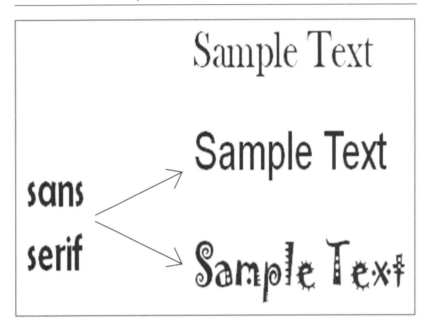

Here again is our focused friend, Baskerville Old Face, starting us off at the top. It is a serif, the first category of type.

The next one down is called Arial. Do you notice how it feels more open and modern? This feeling of openness and modernity comes from the fact that Arial is a sans serif font. Notice how its ends do not taper into smooth feet. The letter shapes cut cleanly off when the letter is sufficiently formed. Now that you are looking closely, you can see how these two types contrast.

This last font is sure fun. It is also a sans serif called Jokerman. To me, its personality says *Fajitas Tonight* and there are situations where that reflection is exactly appropriate and fits your topic, your client, or your project very well. But you clearly do not want to use it on anything longer than just a couple of words. It is way too annoying to read at any considerable length and would likely lead to abandonment, which is when readers simply give up on reading and move on to something else.

Slab Serif

So, I may have told you a small white lie earlier. There are more than two types of type. Lots more. Ask your favorite font nerd. For our purposes, we stick to the basics here, but I think you can handle the introduction of one more type of type, now that you are familiar with the first two.

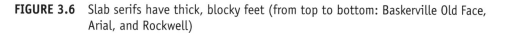

FIGURE 3.6 Slab serifs have thick, blocky feet (from top to bottom: Baskerville Old Face, Arial, and Rockwell)

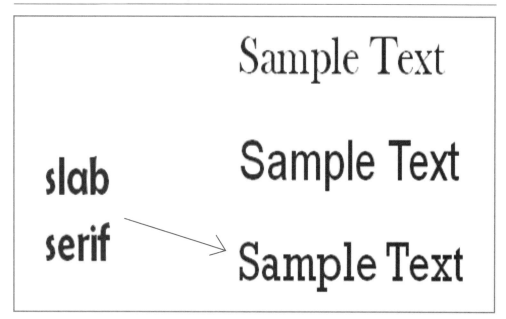

The font at the bottom is known as a slab serif. This particular slab serif is called Rockwell. As points of comparison, I carried over the serif, Baskerville Old Face, and the sans serif, Arial, from earlier. Rockwell is similar to Baskerville Old Face in that it has those little feet . . . actually, those feet are quite large. They do not gradually narrow to a graceful finish like the serifs in Baskerville Old Face. The feet on a slab serif are thick and squared off. Rockwell, the slab serif, is also similar to Arial in that the lines making up the letters are of an even thickness. According to these characteristics, slab serifs are really their own type of type. How would you use Rockwell? Is it suitable for reading at length like the serif fonts? Or is it better on a heading, where more freedom and shorter passages are standard? Here's a quick behind-the-scenes way to answer those questions within your own computer.

What Am I Looking at Here?

To illustrate, this book uses two fonts: a serif called UsherwoodStd-Medium set in 9.5 point size for the narrative text, and a sans serif called OfficinaSansStd-Bold set in 13 point size for the first-level headings, and set in 12 point size for the second-level headings. The decorative font used on the front cover is Myriad Pro.

Every computer has a Fonts folder, but the path to get there and the amount of details you find may vary. This example is what the folder looks like on my PC, running Windows 7.

FIGURE 3.7 This screenshot shows the details about each installed font

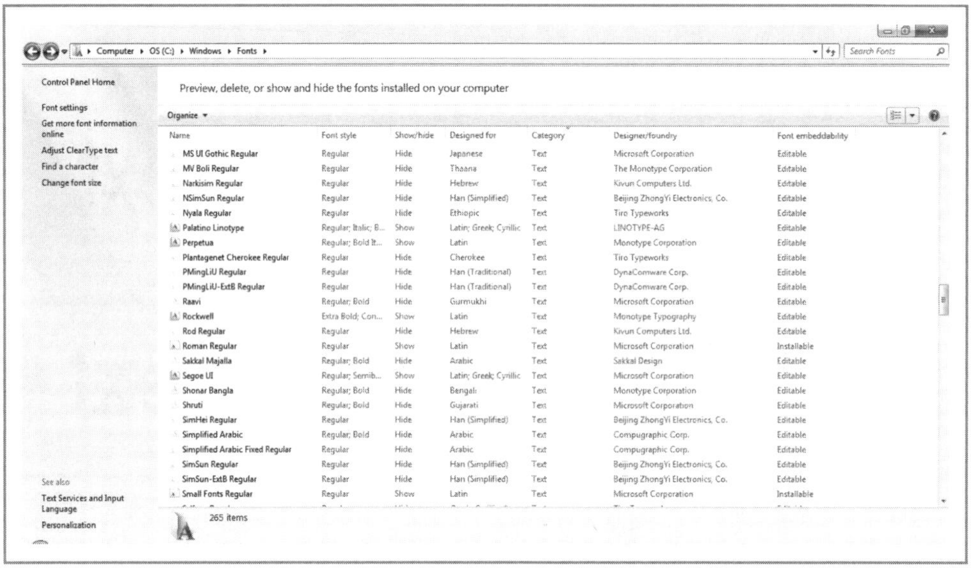

At the top you can see my navigational path. I opened my *C* drive, then my *Windows* folder, and then the *Fonts* folder. Usually the fonts in the Fonts folder are presented as little icons. Change the setting using the dropdown arrow in the upper right to specify the *Details* setting. So many cool details! There are the names of the foundry I envisioned, where someone is sitting at a desk playing with the curvatures on lowercase *t*'s! See the column called Category? Here, the operating system indicates the foundry's recommendation for the best use for the typeface.

This screenshot is showing some of the text fonts (I told you it would make sense later)—these are the ones suitable for long narrative reading, and there is Rockwell. Scrolling down a bit reveals other categories, including one called *Display*.

Display fonts are those fonts created to be used as titles, headings, and with report elements of that nature. They are also suitable for use in slideshows, where the text is somewhat sparse and heading-like. Checking the Fonts folder is an immediate way to diagnose proper font usage.

In general, graphic designers suggest you pick two or maybe three fonts for your entire piece of work. Every operating system contains grips of fonts that you probably do not ever need in your professional reporting. There are font categories called *Script* and *Decorative*.

On occasion, and on a single letter, or on one or two words in a title, these types of type might be appropriate, but generally err on the side of legibility.

What Works for Paper and What Works for Screen?

Aside from being a useful way to add visual interest to a written page, sans serif fonts are also critical for electronic projection, whether on a computer screen or a slide projector.

Serif fonts like Baskerville Old Face do not work well with an electronic screen. Go back and check out Figure 3.6. Notice how Baskerville Old Face shows variation within the line of each letter? Look at the *m* in Sample. The line is much thinner at the top of the bumps. That thick-thin line variation makes it very difficult to read serif fonts on the screen. The thin parts of the letters almost disappear, even when the type is greatly enlarged. For electronic screens, use sans serif fonts, which tend to be an even thickness. Compare the *m* in the Arial example; the thick-thin line variation is gone. Now, check out Rockwell, the third font shown. Slab serifs also do not have that thick-thin line variation, so they are easier to read on a screen.

Therefore, when writing a report that will only be read on computer screens (this is more and more common as companies go paperless), use a sans or slab serif. Onscreen legibility tests (e.g., Chaparro, Shaikh, Chaparro, & Merkle, 2010) suggest Franklin Gothic, Cambria, Verdana, and Consolas are good choices, because they produce fewer errors in character recognition. As an example, character recognition matters when needing to distinguish a zero from a lowercase o, or a numeral 1 from an uppercase I or a lowercase l.

Slideshow templates do not always follow these guidelines. At this moment, almost a quarter of the default font choices preloaded into the templates on my computer identify a serif font for the main slide headings, which I think holds too much thick-thin line variation to maintain legibility. If you choose to use a slide template, remember that you are in control of it. You can change the font choices, make the fonts larger, and manipulate them so that it becomes a clearer package for your data.

Changing up the font choice to match the dissemination method is how we arrive at the recommendation of using three fonts per project. The slideshow usually has two—a sans or slab serif for the headings and a different sans or slab serif for the little bits of other content on the slide. But the handout that you distribute to your audience members containing your key points should have a serif (the third font in your package), because the data there is communicated as narrative text.

The headings or callout points on your handout can be set in the slab or sans serif used in your slides. A similar heading font, plus the repetition of other elements we talk about like color and graphics, makes it obvious that your materials belong together, represents you as a polished professional, and helps your audience engage with your content. Now that you know the basic rules about typeface, you are equipped to make informed decisions about which types of type to use where and when.

What About Web Fonts?

Typeface for the web should not have that thick-thin line variation that I have been deriding for the bulk of this chapter. They are on-screen, after all, so we probably need a sans serif or at least a serif with pretty evenly thick lines. However, in many cases these days, web fonts also must be recognized by any user's computer. That sure limits things! Very few fonts are universal. Now, Georgia (a serif) and Verdana (a sans serif) were both designed specifically for the screen and for use at small or large sizes. They would seem like great choices for websites. But, while they are widely distributed fonts, they are not installed everywhere.

FIGURES 3.8 and 3.9 Sans serif (top) and serif (bottom) versions of my blog

In the figures above, the version of my blog in Figure 3.8 uses a sans serif, which is easier to read on screen. The version in Figure 3.9 shows the same post in a serif, Adobe Caslon Pro. Even though it is popular for its elegance on paper, notice how much smaller and harder it is to read the serif.

For this reason, programming code for webpages usually calls on an entire font backup plan. You can usually leave this task up to your IT person (oh wait, are you also your organization's IT person?), but you want to be sure a readable, web-appropriate font like Verdana or Georgia is listed first in the code, with other solid backup choices listed after that. My blog's font family consists of Segoe UI, Helvetica, Arial, sans serif—which basically lists my preferred order of display. A family of backup choices on hand helps ensure that your content is readable, regardless of the specific fonts installed on your site visitors' computers. In the very near future, font files will be embedded within a site and independent from an end user's font files. We expect to see a much larger set of web font choices, though for legibility stick to sans or slab serifs. In the meantime, do check how your site copy looks in each font in your family to make certain that changes in the display do not affect your formatting.

How Can I Protect Font Choices?

I used all of those rules and guidelines when I designed the report I detailed at the start of this chapter—still, everything went awry. Let's break down what happened.

I set the report's narrative type in Gentium Book Basic, a typeface installed on my workplace PC. Gentium Book Basic is a decent font, holds up well on screen, yet it is a serif that can be read at length. Sounds like a superstar, right? But, when I shipped the report out to my boss, he opened it at home on his Macintosh, where that font was not in his font book. Oh, the trials and tribulations of PC-Mac compatibility!

His Mac did not recognize my font (or the one I used on the headings), so it executed a font substitution and replaced Gentium Book Basic with another font so that my boss could read it. Oftentimes, computers do not even let their owners know that a font substitution has been made. So when he opened the file, he presumed that what he saw was the product of an employee he knew cared a lot about font choices and assumed it was my preference for it to look that way.

It is painful to go to all the trouble of selecting the perfect font, only to have it substituted when the report electronically leaves your hands. You might be tempted to think that this is why the PDF format was invented, right? Don't be fooled. PDF does not completely cure your font substitution ills, particularly when working with a PC-Mac translation. Nor does it make document cocreation any easier when producing data presentations as a team.

In those cases where the whole team is working in a PC environment, here is what I know now about document protection that I did not know then. Embed the fonts.

In Word 2010, you can automatically embed your fonts when you save.

FIGURE 3.10 This screenshot shows a typical Save window—notice the arrow between the word Tools and the Save button

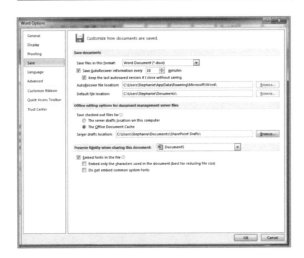

Before hitting that *Save* button, click the dropdown arrow next to *Tools* and choose the *Save Options* link. That opens up a popup box that looks like this:

FIGURE 3.11 The bottom set of checkboxes shows where you can adjust the settings related to embedding your font

Then, make certain that the checkbox next to *Embed fonts in the file* is activated. Now, the font files travel with the document as it is disseminated. Your readers cannot download the font to their own computers, but they are able to read your materials the way you intended them to look. You can also ensure that the fonts are embedded for all new documents by choosing that option from the dropdown menu, which, in this screenshot, says Document 5. However, be careful—in my experience, embedding the fonts can raise the file size by about 25%.

You can navigate the same path to embed fonts in any Office 2010 program on PCs. This way, you do not have to worry about your fonts getting substituted as you distribute your work or when you plug your flash drive into another computer.

PC-Mac compatibility is a little trickier, as Macs do not always recognize PC font embedding. In those cases, you can send the font to your colleague and have her download it to her Mac (I have included instructions online for this). If the recipient is a client or professor, where it can be awkward to ask them to download and install a font, then stick with fonts common to both computer types, such as Baskerville, Arial (PC)/Helvetica (Mac), or Calibri. As one final possibility, if you want to use uncommon fonts minimally (as we discuss next), you can type those words into text boxes, then copy the text box and paste it again right into the document as a picture file. That is a pain, of course, so be selective about the use of non-standard fonts.

How Do Fonts Actually Communicate?

Psychologists debate the exact details, but we know that the eye-brain connection does not work by reading through each individual letter (Pelli, Farell, & Moore, 2003). Rather, curves of letters and the composure of ascenders (think of the tall sticks on an h) and descenders (think of the stick that hangs down on a y) influence recognition of an entire word. As such, fonts deserve our thoughtful attention because of their impact on our readers.

Beyond the words they compose, the individual characteristics that differentiate one font from the next also communicate subtle messages to the audience (Lewis & Walker, 1989). Sometimes, this is obvious: fonts that look like handwriting convey that the content is more informal or youthful, without the audience ever reading a single word.

Take, for example, these slides starting off a discussion on student enrollment within a History Department.

The title slide in Figure 3.12 is from a PowerPoint template. The default font in the template, Tw Cen MT, is a sans serif—good for screen reading, yes, but it can send a mixed message to the audience. The font may be too modern for a history department. Hang in there with me while I explain. Figure 3.13 is the same content in another PowerPoint template, this time set in Book Antigua, a serif font. Notice how Book Antigua feels more classic, more appropriate for the fine folks in History? It is more fitting for the subject, but serif is not great for screen reading. What a dilemma.

FIGURES 3.12 and 3.13   Two template-based slides, one modern (on the left) with a sans serif font and one more classic (on the right) with a serif font

FIGURE 3.14   Selected words can be set in a decorative, mood-setting font, while the rest of the text supports readability

A much friendlier option is to use the power of highly communicative fonts to set off a single word. Highlighting just one word or phrase still influences the flavor of the content and represents the subject well, as long as the surrounding fonts are somewhat neutral. In the revision in Figure 3.14, I used another standard PowerPoint template where the default font is Arial Black, but I offset one word using a more decorative font with an aged look, called Blackadder. Now, we solved the issues of finding a representative font that communicates the subject and locating a font that reads well on screen. The trick, however, is to restrict the use of the decorative font. Notice in the next example how the overuse completely obliterates the impact and even the legibility (that title actually says "KCC Enrollment Over Time").

FIGURE 3.15   Overuse of the decorative font destroys good design and legibility

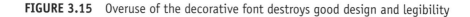

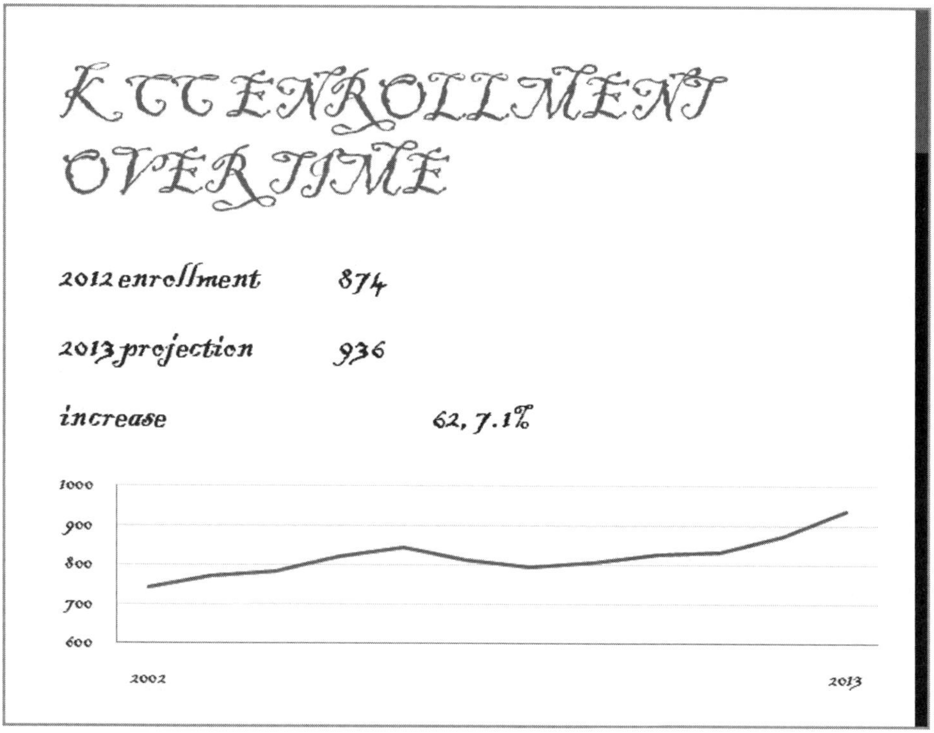

The best way to offset a single word or two is through the use of an extra text box. Definitely, you can keep KCC History Department in one text box and just change the font on History, but that type of change throws off line spacing, especially if you increase the size of the highlighted word, as I did here. Insert>Text box as needed.

Let's look at one more example.

FIGURE 3.16 Research poster that communicates credibility

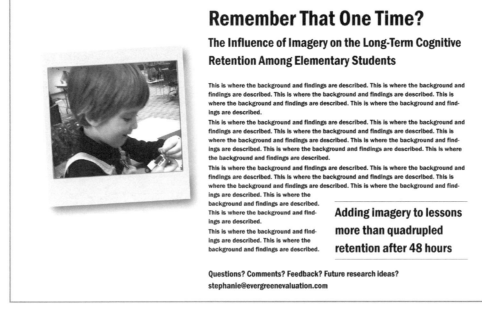

FIGURE 3.17 Same poster, just a different font—one that communicates immaturity

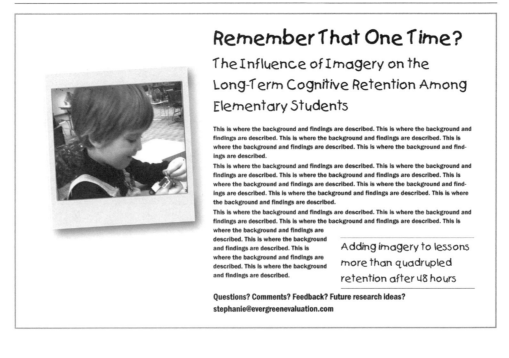

In the selections, same research, same poster layout, just two very different display fonts. The display font (used on the title, subtitle, and callout) for the poster in Figure 3.16 is set in Franklin Gothic Demi Condensed. By contrast, the display font used in the poster in Figure 3.17 is called Kids.

Now, we just discussed the need for appropriately matching font personalities to their subject matter, right? By that logic, at first glance it is easy to assume that Kids is the correct font to choose for the research presented on the poster. Yet the Kids font does a disservice to the research—and, by proxy, the researcher. It communicates a personality of playfulness and immaturity and it is these characteristics that are interpreted by the onlookers. In addition to impairing legibility, notice how difficult it is to read through and digest the entire subtitle; the font subtly undermines the credibility of the authors. (Let me say that as a former early childhood specialist and current parent, kid-print typefaces also do not belong on newsletters, lunch calendars, report cards, or classroom walls. They neither model proper letter formation for children nor adequately represent the professionalism and respectability of the teaching field.) Do you think applying the Kids font on a single word in the title is effective here? Maybe I have just been overexposed to the kid-print font, but I would say fonts like these have no place in professional reporting situations.

The more serious display font in Figure 3.17 is not a serif, which traditionally tends to come off as more professional and classic than the sans serif I used, which is clear and crisp and condensed—everything we want on a research poster. It is a better reflection of the competency of the research team, and it is this match between the font and the research that is more appropriate. The child-focused aspect of the study is effectively presented through the picture. The font here represents the integrity of the work.

How Big Should I Make My Narrative Typeface?

Did you know that you regularly read type set in size 8, or even smaller? In printed materials, captions and less important information (think: photograph credits, newsletter headline subtext, magazine staff listings) are usually reduced to something between 7.5 to 9 points. Additionally, we generally read that size type without much issue. The reason why we can comfortably read those small sizes is because the designers chose an effective font that keeps its clarity and legibility when shrunk. The fonts in Figure 3.18 are all set in 9-point size.

FIGURE 3.18   Six common fonts set in 9-point size

In order of appearance, they are

Baskerville Old Face

Corbel

Times New Roman

Cambria

Palatino Linotype

Verdana

Sample Text

Sample Text

Sample Text

Sample Text

Sample Text

Sample Text

Comparatively, they do not hold up equally well. Our good friend Baskerville Old Face is too tiny to read at 9-point size, and here is why. Without getting into too much typographic anatomy details, look at the short height of the lowercase letters. Compare the lowercase *t* at the end of text set in Baskerville Old Face with the lowercase *t* set in the next font down, Corbel. See how much taller the lowercase Corbel *t* looks when compared to Baskerville Old Face? While they are all set in 9-point size, graphic designers describe the Corbel typeface as having what they call a taller x-height (named, cleverly, after the size of the lowercase x). For our purposes here, the point is simply that the other options below Baskerville Old Face are taller, making them more legible. Some, such as the last one, Verdana, are also wider, which is helpful for those of us who get headaches from squinting too much. But, what works at 9-point size does not always work at larger point sizes. Check out your nearest magazine. Chances are that the small-size captions are set in a different typeface than the larger text intended for narrative reading.

Guiding Idea

Long reading is in 9 to 11 point's

FIGURE 3.19   Same six common fonts set in 11-point size

Sample Text

Sample Text

Sample Text

Sample Text

Sample Text

Sample Text

Speaking strictly of narrative prose in print, size 11 is about right. Studies show that 11-point text is easiest to read at length, but as usual, it depends on the typeface. Here, in Figure 3.19, we have the same fonts, enlarged to 11 points. Baskerville Old Face is still too tiny for me, because the holes in the lowercase e's are not yet visible (okay fine, font nerds, the *bowl* in the lowercase e!). Any of the next four fonts in the list look good. Verdana, the last one, looks a bit too large, doesn't it? Text that is too large looks immature. If you love Verdana, just set it in 10 point.

Let's return to the distinction between print and web for a moment. The default type size in Microsoft Word used to be 12 points (set in Times New Roman). This looked appropriate as we typed on screen, but when printed it tended to look large and unprofessional. Currently, the type size default in Word is 11 points (and it is set in Calibri), which functions well for printed materials. On the web, a larger font size is typically desired. Standard, reliable choices are Verdana, set in 12 points, or Arial/Helvetica, set in 13 points. Of course, when it comes to the font you choose in your dissertation, use whatever is mandated.

How Large Should I Make My Heading Typeface?

We are now moving up in size, looking at the same group of typefaces set in 18 points: a size more suitable for headings or titles in printed materials. Generally speaking, headings should be made 150% to 200% of the body text size. So, if the narrative text is set in 11, the headings should be set in something between 16 and 22 points. At this size, any of the typefaces are legible and appropriate. Choose the upper end of this spectrum for the title and then scale back in size from there for headings, and even more for subheadings so that their size falls into the lower end of the spectrum.

Audiences interpret larger size as higher importance. In a hierarchy of information, largest is at the top. Varying type size communicates the organizational structure of the report and provides the reader with clues to the author's logic.

Outside of reports, 18-point size is also common for use on the narrative portion of poster text. At that size, it can be read comfortably from about 2.5 feet away. Of course, none of the options we discussed so far are suitable for poster headings or slide decks. But that is okay. We present data effectively. We're flexible.

Poster headings and the bits of text you include on slides should be set in about 40-point size or larger. Text at this size is legible from more than 5 feet. This means conference attendees can read your research poster title from down the aisle and come in closer to examine the details. Using the same group of typefaces shown in Figure 3.21, but set in 40 point, we can

FIGURE 3.20 Same six fonts in 18-point size—more appropriate for headings

Sample Text
Sample Text
Sample Text
Sample Text
Sample Text
Sample Text

POSTER

FIGURE 3.21 Same fonts set in slideshow size—40 point

Sample Text
Sample Text
Sample Text
Sample Text
Sample Text
Sample Text

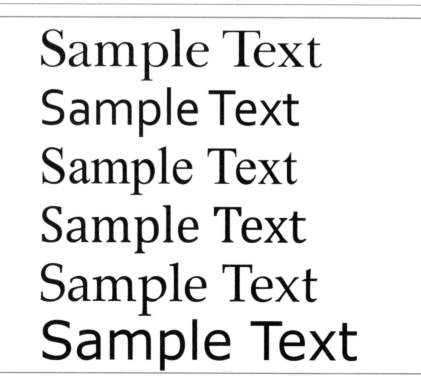

see that they do not hold up equally well at large sizes. In particular, the serif fonts tend to fall apart, with their thinner parts getting so thin that they begin to impact legibility. Corbel and Verdana, the two sans serif fonts, are crisper and clearer.

Poster titles, on the other hand, are often as large as 150 points, which allows someone to read it from about 25 feet away. That large a size is also useful for slide deck text, particularly when presenting your research in a cavernous room. This means the folks sitting in the back row of your conference session or your classroom lecture hall stay more engaged and less annoyed.

You can get a rough idea of whether your slideshow's type size is sufficiently large by using the slide sorter view. In PowerPoint, it looks like this:

FIGURE 3.22 This screenshot of the slide sorter view is a quick way of getting a sense of how your text looks to the audience members in the back row of a medium-size room

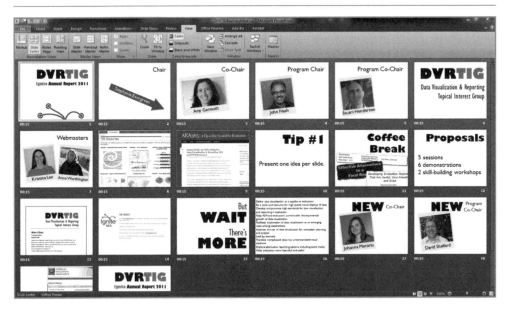

If you can read your words in the slide sorter mode, then chances are good that so can the audience in your presentation room.

To verify your size on a PC, click on the *View* tab and look to the left for *Slide Sorter* in the *Presentation View* group. In case you are wondering, the largest type displayed is set in 115 point in Gill Sans Ultra Bold. The smaller text is from the same typeface family—Gills Sans MT, but in size 44. Slide 16 has lots of text crammed in at size 28, which may be too small. But, of course, the point of that slide was to create an overwhelming feeling.

Guiding Idea

Line spacing is 11 to 13 points

If the text is too small, and enlarging it is impossible because there is too much text on the slide, guess what? It means there is too much text on the slide. Break those points apart so that each one has its own slide.

How Should Lines Be Spaced?

Before we get too much further, let's chat for a moment about a closely related issue. Line spacing (i.e., the distance between lines within a paragraph) can still impact legibility, even when effective fonts are selected.

For lines within a paragraph, generally choose line spacing that is 1 to 2 points larger than the body text. In Word, this can be done in two ways. Clicking on *Line Spacing Options* in the drop-down arrow in the *Paragraph* area of the *Home* tab opens up the box shown in Figure 3.23.

FIGURE 3.23   This window is where you can adjust the spacing between the lines of narrative text

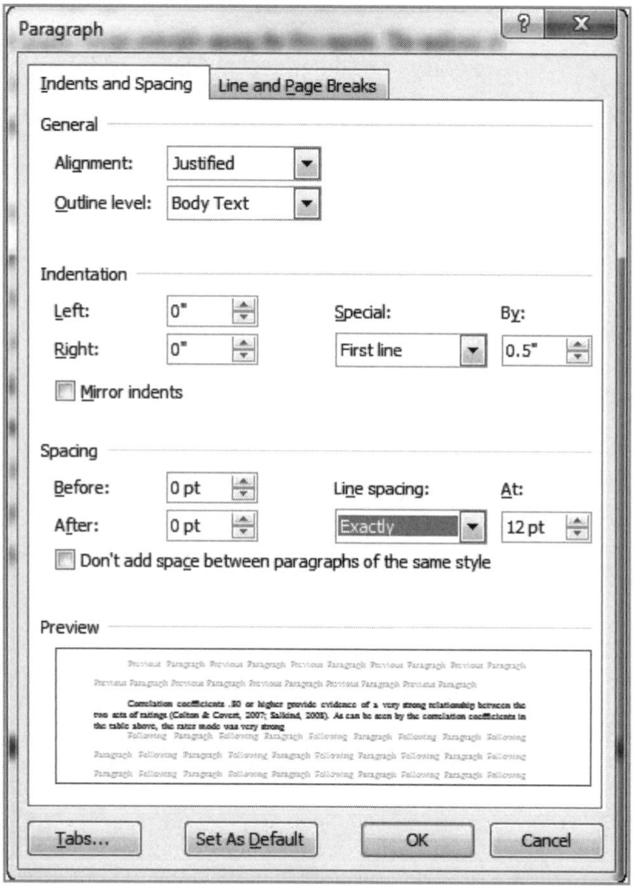

From the highlighted dropdown menu called *Line Spacing*, you can choose *Exactly* and type in something between 11 and 13. Alternatively, you can choose *Multiple* and type in something between 1.1 and 1.2, going down with lots of decimal places available there.

FIGURE 3.24 Three line spacing possibilities, each influencing the readability of the text

11 point text 11 point spacing **Too narrow!**	Generally speaking, ideal reading conditions occur when the line spacing within a paragraph is set 1-2 points larger than the size of the text itself. If you know your type size, you can figure out proper line spacing.
11 point text 13 point spacing **I can breathe!**	Generally speaking, ideal reading conditions occur when the line spacing within a paragraph is set 1-2 points larger than the size of the text itself. If you know your type size, you can figure out proper line spacing.
11 point text 22 point spacing **I'm lost in space!!**	Generally speaking, ideal reading conditions occur when the line spacing within a paragraph is set 1-2 points larger than the size of the text itself. If you know your type size, you can figure out proper line spacing.

When the lines are too close together, the ascenders from one line bump into the descenders from another line, making it difficult to discern the words and causing general feelings of claustrophobia. Line spacing that is too far apart, as in the last instance in the figure above, breaks up the fluidity of the paragraph.

How Does Typeface Help Organize Data Presentation?

A change in font indicates a change in meaning and invites the audience to spend energy to interpret the meaning. This is why unnecessary font changes—whether in the font itself or in the size—cause audience frustration. So, be intentional about font changes and only incorporate them when you want to signal a shift in the narrative, such as the start of a new section or the title to a chart. Here are five places where a font change is warranted (we discuss a few others later on in the context of data displays): headings, callouts, sidebars, quotes, and bullets.

Guiding Idea

No more than three fonts are used

Headings

Headings are a clue to the report's organization. They can be distinguished from body text by their placement above the narrative and they can be further distinguished through the use of a font change. When moving between fonts, make them very different. If the sans serif heading looks too similar to the serif body type, it just comes off as a sloppy mistake. Be a little bold with the headings. Contrast with body text by using a different font category, size, style, and/or color. Looks that are too similar seem unintentional.

Subheadings are set in the same font as the document's headings. In keeping with a hierarchical organization, the subheadings should just be downplayed a bit: smaller in size than the headings, or a more neutral color, or italicized.

Callouts

Callout boxes are those short bursts of text that highlight a key point from the research. They are usually embedded within the narrative text; however, because they are used for emphasis, they must be visibly distinguished from the narrative text. In terms of content hierarchy, headings are more important than callouts, and callouts are more important than the narrative.

For example, in the research poster we dissected earlier in this chapter, the callout box in the lower right was set in 72-point size—the same size as the subtitle, and both are smaller than the main title.

FIGURE 3.25   Callout boxes can be distinguished from the narrative text by adjusting type settings, such as size and font

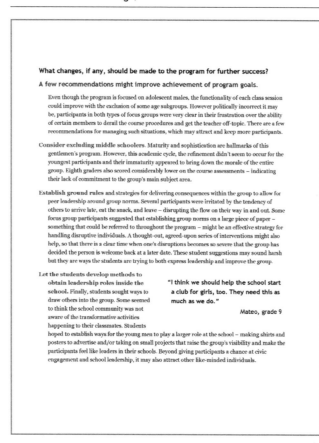

In the report page shown here, the callout box is emphasized by its distinction from the narrative text. First, it is set in the same font as the heading—Trebuchet—so that it is visually

different from the narrative, indicating to the reader that there is a change in meaning taking place. Second, the callout box has an ample margin separating it from the narrative text. It is also larger, set at 12 points rather than 11. The APA Guide (2010) recommends that figures and sidebars should be set in a sans serif font, at a size between 8 and 14 points. All of those settings then create a situation where the callout box is lifted out of the narrative to become higher in the hierarchy of importance on the page.

Sidebars

Shifts in the narrative also occur with the introduction of sidebars. Sidebars are a way to showcase a short poignant story or to describe a detail that is related but not a direct part of the narrative. The conceptual distinction needs to be physically presented in the report via a sidebar.

FIGURE 3.26 Sidebars are a good place to introduce a third font

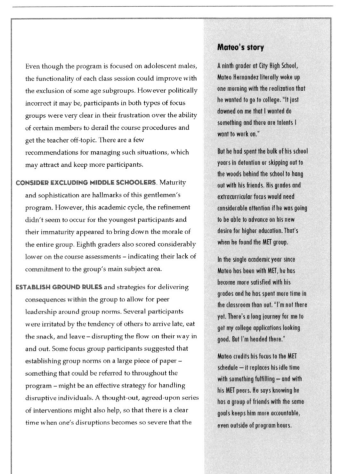

This example shows a sidebar that contains a small success case study. The content can stand on its own and serves as a complement to the narrative, making it suitable material for a sidebar. The sidebar is established with a gray background, and while color is commonly used to demarcate separate space, it is not totally necessary. As we discuss in the color chapter, be careful that the sidebar background color is light enough for good legibility.

What is more compulsory is that the sidebar content is set in a different font, in order to not confuse it with the narrative text. In fact, sidebars are frequently set in a third font, not the one used for the text or the headings of the report. Often, the third font is a sans serif that complements the other two. Identifying three complementary fonts can be tricky. There are some font-matching resources at the end of this chapter, but as a backup plan you can set the sidebar in the same font as your sans serif report heading and get the job done. Be attentive to the line length here—I used a condensed font for the sidebar to get closer to the ideal of 8 to12 words per line, which is discussed in Chapter 5 on arrangement.

Quotes

Stylistic uniformity means that each narrative text section has normal text in sentence case. No bolded words. No all caps. Nothing underlined. In essence, if you blur your eyes just a bit, the narrative text should look like a gray blob with nothing in particular standing out or emphasized. Stylistic uniformity supports undistracted and speedier reading.

Guiding Idea

Body text has stylistic uniformity

We talk about quantitative data displays at the end of each chapter, but we have not discussed how to display qualitative data very much. There are some cool ways (getting even cooler by the day) to visualize qualitative data, but for now, that is beyond the scope of this book. The most basic way to show qualitative data is through the quotes of our research participants. *Do not put the quotes in italics.* That's funny. But, I am serious: Do not put the quotes in italics. Italicized text breaks uniformity. Sure, it draws attention. While it initially draws the eyes, it works against comprehension because italics are hard to read, especially at length. Quotation marks are sufficient to indicate a quote.

When Should I Break the Uniformity Rule?

Of course, uniformity is the ideal, but there are some situations where there is no choice but to emphasize within the narrative text. For example, grant applications, journals, and dissertations are notoriously strict in their text settings, specifying the font and font size and restricting the use of other features like callout boxes. I even worked on a grant for one foundation where the application had to be cut and pasted into text boxes on a website. In these situations, bolding or all caps might be the only option for those critical pieces of text that must stand out to the reader. Because those emphasis methods can make it hard to read text, be judicious with your use.

I know it probably sounds like certain of my recommendations make data presentation pretty boring. And, given some of the restrictions I outlined, it might seem like you are destined to make the most uninteresting typeface choices. This is actually what we want for our narrative text. We do not want people distracted by the shapes of our letters; we want them reading our letters to digest our data presentation. When the narrative text conveys information we want retained, it is okay to be boring. We have other methods of emphasizing and highlighting our key messages. Additionally, you save yourself the time and effort of styling the text. Uniformity is a win-win for you and your reader.

Bullets

Guiding Idea

Bullets are slightly less thick than text

Personally, I think bullets kill—by that I mean that sometimes they create more problems than they help. Too often, they are used whenever a sentence contains enough objects that it can become a list. Instead of a sentence with 10 commas, authors make a bulleted list; but bullets can be very powerful.

Notice in this example how the darkness of the bullets is nearly the same as the bold heading text? Default bullets are dark. The black dots contrast with the white background more than the text on the slide, and thus they pop out to the reader. The bullets are surrounded by white space, contributing to their emphasis as focal points. Our eyes are drawn to the bullets. That is a lot of power, except we tend to use them on anything that could be a list instead of reserving them for what really needs the reader's attention.

So, I will tell you how to use bullets, if you promise to wield them wisely. If you must use bullets, decrease their size to slightly less (70–80%) than the narrative font point size.

FIGURE 3.27 Bullets are generally too dark and distracting to the eye

FIGURE 3.28 If you must use bullets, lighten them so they are less distracting

Header
Some introductory text goes here
• Lots of information in bullets
• Lots of information in bullets
• Lots of information in bullets
• Lots of information in bullets
Then we continue with more text

Header
Some introductory text goes here
• Lots of information in bullets
• Lots of information in bullets
• Lots of information in bullets
• Lots of information in bullets
Then we continue with more text

It might be a subtle difference, but now the bullets are lighter than the heading and do not compete with the rest of the text for attention. Yet they still contrast enough to serve their purpose of pointing out a subset of important information to the reader.

My preference is to delete the bullets altogether.

A good, strong indentation can cue a reader to a subset of information, possibly as well if not better than the dark circles.

FIGURE 3.29 Adequate indentation can achieve the same effect as bullets

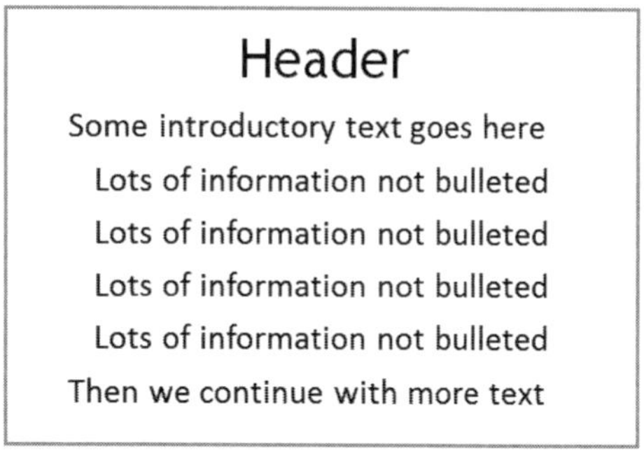

Header
Some introductory text goes here
Lots of information not bulleted
Lots of information not bulleted
Lots of information not bulleted
Lots of information not bulleted
Then we continue with more text

How Do I Apply These Ideas to Graphs?

Compared to the other chapters in this book, the font tends to play the smallest role in good data visualization. Most of the time, our concerns about a graph's text are about removing the excess so that the graph is less cluttered. Also, variation in font size is an effective and underutilized method to support clarity in data visualizations.

As you now know, fonts can help establish a hierarchy of importance within a data display. The most important part of the graph, usually its title, should be the largest in size to draw a viewer's attention first. Notice also that the title is written like a headline with a key takeaway point.

FIGURE 3.30 Changes in font size within a graph title can communicate primary and secondary importance

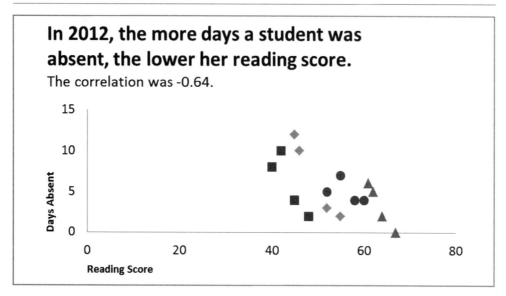

In 2012, the more days a student was absent, the lower her reading score.
The correlation was -0.64.
15
10
5
0
Days Absent
0
20
40
60
80
Reading Score

Can Text Sit on an Angle?

Observe that some of the graphs in this section contain axis labels that are oriented at a 90-degree angle. There is debate about whether angled text is acceptable. Designers tend to believe it looks prettier, more aligned with the axis itself. People concerned with legibility claim that the severe angle makes the text hard to read. I am comfortable with the threat to legibility here, because it is just an axis label. However, 90-degree text should not be used on the labels in the x axis, because it damages both the design and legibility. In that case, I have seen 45-degree angled text used successfully, when necessary. All of this talk becomes a nonissue, though, if the data is commonly viewed on a smartphone. Sideways or slanted text invites the smartphone holder to tilt the phone so that the text can be read straight at 0 degrees. However, if you tilt a smartphone it causes its internal mechanisms to tilt the view and the viewer cannot read the text at 0 degrees unless she steadies the phone and tilts her head. If your data presentation is going to be read on a smartphone, do not angle the text.

Guiding Idea

Headings and callouts are emphasized

What is the next most important part of the display to capture the audience's attention? In the example above, it is the subtitle, which further interprets and explains the data. Thus, the subtitle is smaller in size than the title but larger than the text labeling the axes. In some cases, graph designers like to exchange a subtitle for an annotation, and they might plunk a callout box right next to a key point in a graph. These annotations should be treated the same as subtitles, in terms of the font size hierarchy.

FIGURE 3.31   Font size helps establish a hierarchy within a data display

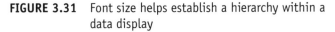

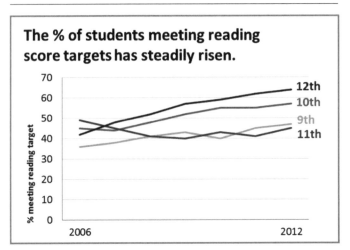

In the case of Figure 3.31, with no descriptive subtitle, the data labels at the end of each line fill the second position in the importance hierarchy. They are still a larger size than the values along the y axis or the axis label. In some cases, even with the addition of a descriptive subtitle, it may be appropriate that the data labels remain second in importance. If so, the title of the graph would be largest, then the data labels, then the descriptive subtitle, then the supporting axis text. You can even increase the size of a single data label, if that was an area that needed the most attention from the audience. Changes in size catch early attention.

Just do not forget about the fact that the graph is usually embedded into a document that has surrounding text. If, for example, a report heading is on the same page, the report heading may supersede the graph heading in importance, shifting everything in your data display hierarchy down a step. Always choose data visualization text sizes within the context of your larger reporting medium.

What Is the Bottom Line?

Choices in font category, size, and spacing affect legibility and influence the mood or environment of the reporting, as well as reflect the competence of the researcher. A hierarchy of importance, established by controlling and manipulating the font, communicates to the reader the desired focus and order for attention. Thus, font choices should be deliberate and consistent. Consistency in our presentations increases legibility and comprehension of our data.

KEY POINTS TO REMEMBER

Typefaces communicate message and intent on their own, regardless of the actual words typed in the typeface.

- Legibility is impacted by the font. Generally, serif fonts are best for long narrative reading on paper. Fonts with an even thickness to their letter shapes—usually sans serifs—are better for on-screen reading.

- Check the details about the fonts installed on your own computer for a better understanding of their intended use.

- Mood is also influenced by font choices. Serifs are perceived as more traditional and serious. More playful decorative fonts are useful to communicate a more obvious mood, but use them sparingly because they generally hurt legibility.

- Font size also sends a message. Importance is signaled by size so that the most important things are the largest, decreasing in size as the significance of the displayed text decreases. Supportive text like captions can be set in something teeny like 8 points. By contrast, titles of research posters can be set as large as 150 points, to accommodate reading from a distance.

- If bullets must be used, decrease their size so that they are less distracting.

- Lines of text that are too narrow or too far apart impact readability, even if you have chosen a beautiful font. For narrative reading, adjust line spacing so it is 1 to 3 points larger than the size of the text.

HOW CAN I EXTEND THIS?

Check Out

What the Font? at (http://www.myfonts.com/WhatTheFont/)—Have you ever seen a cool font and wondered what it is? Snap a picture or a screenshot and upload it to What the Font? This website looks for indicators and characteristics of certain fonts and churns out its best guess as to the font in question. (The site's main purpose is to then sell that font to the user, but you do not have to take it that far.)

Fontpark at (http://fontpark.net/en/)—Graphic designers will not be happy that I am pointing out free font sites—they tend to think you should purchase full-type families from the typeface foundry and that fonts on free sites are a bit junky. Well, there may be some truth to that sentiment, but I still find Fontpark a great place to locate fonts, especially slightly funky ones to pop out certain words in my titles. Be certain to watch the licensing here since some say commercial and some are listed as noncommercial.

Font Squirrel at (http://www.fontsquirrel.com/)—All fonts on this site are free for commercial use. If you locate one you like, you can take some sample text for a test drive. But read the license agreement carefully—it may require that you only distribute documents with the font to third parties as a PDF. Regardless, embed your font! Embed your font!

10 Typeface Pairs for Cash Poor Designers at (http://morganelye.com/?p=433)—That's us. These heading-body text pairings pull from the default fonts for PCs and Macs.

A Little Can Go A Long Way at (http://www.smashingmagazine.com/2010/12/14/what-font-should-i-use-five-principles-for-choosing-and-using-typefaces/)—This article from Smashing Magazine has a lot of great advice, but pay particular attention to Point 4, where they depict the practice of using decorative fonts selectively.

The Errol Morris Font Experiment at (http://opinionator.blogs.nytimes.com/2012/08/08/hear-all-ye-people-hearken-o-earth/)—In the ruse that was published in his *New York Times* column, Morris randomly displayed some text in six varying fonts and provided evidence that text set in Baskerville was viewed as more trustworthy. See the experimental column and read his debriefing.

Try This

As in the History Department example shown earlier, changing fonts for a single word can have a big impact on the look and feel of a page or slide. Open up the report you are currently working on or the last one you finished, identify the keyword or two, and match it with a font that resonates with your subject matter. You may have to paste your emphasis words into their own text box to make this work.

Take a moment now to define your personal style. Pick your own heading and body font. Choose something that represents you well. Save the theme (see the last chapter) and name it after yourself. Of course, there may be times when your personal branding choices need downplaying in the service of blending in with someone else's branding, such as a client, a department, or a funder.

Send font pairs on a date at Type Connection at http://www.typeconnection.com/. This site lets you test the font-pairing waters through a matchmaking game. If you are a nerd, you will enjoy the step that illustrates the reasons why certain fonts pair well together. Most fonts in the game are not native to PCs, but you can always look for the ones you like at the font-finding websites listed above.

WHERE CAN I GO FOR MORE INFORMATION?

American Psychological Association. (2010). *Publication Manual of the American Psychological Association* (6th ed.). Washington, DC: Author.

Chaparro, B. S., Shaikh, A. D., Chaparro, A., & Merkle, E. C. (2010). Comparing the legibility of six ClearType typefaces to Verdana and Times New Roman. *Information Design Journal, 18*(1), 36–49.

Lewis, C., & Walker, P. (1989). Typographic influences on reading. *British Journal of Psychology, 80*, 241–257.

Lupton, E. (2004). Thinking with type: A critical guide for designers, writers, editors, and students. New York: Princeton Architectural Press.

Modern Language Association of America. (2009). *MLA handbook for writers of research papers* (7th ed.). New York: Author.

Pelli, D. G., Farell, B., & Moore, D. C. (2003). The remarkable inefficiency of word recognition. *Nature, 423*, 752–756.

Song, H., & Schwartz, N. (2008). If it's hard to read, it's hard to do: Processing fluency affects effort prediction and motivation. *Psychological Science, 19*(10), 986–988.

Wheildon, C. (2005). *Type & layout: Are you communicating or just making pretty shapes?* Victoria, Australia: The Worsley Press.

CHAPTER 4

Color

Learning Objectives

After reading this chapter you will be able to:

- Identify the basic colors needed for optimal reading
- Pull colors out of an image
- Build a color scheme
- Replicate colors in standard software
- Distinguish between applying color for decoration or emphasis
- Check for legibility in different environments
- Apply color to data for emphasis

Before we advance any further, this book exemplifies the difficult task of writing a chapter about color for a book that is printed in two colors only. All images in this chapter are also located in full color online at www.sagepub.com/evergreen and I strongly encourage you to head there to get a more complete picture.

As before, let's begin with another cathartic story about how I learned a big lesson on use of color.

I made Figure 4.1 (it was not my finest hour) as part of a report I submitted several years ago. Visualize it in the default rainbow color scheme of Excel, where reading from the top, each line is blue, red, green, purple, and teal. As was my typical process, I made the report in color, and I then translated it into a PDF file and sent it to the main contact person at my client's office. Some of you are probably using a similar

Guiding Ideas

Narrative text is dark gray or black

Background has white or subdued color

One or two emphasis colors are used

Color reprints legibly in black and white

Color changes denote meaning changes

FIGURE 4.1   Line graph made with Excel's default colors

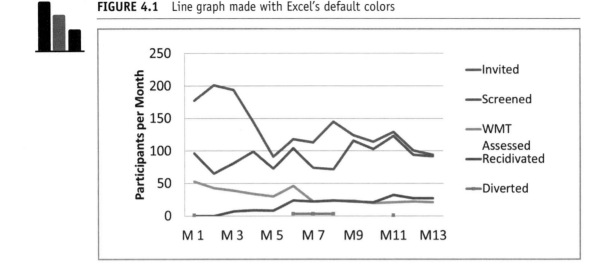

process to submit papers to your professor, or status updates to your supervisor. And as was her typical process, she printed it on her office printer (in this case, a black-and-white printer) and then made copies of that printout for the other panelists to review.

When I arrived a few weeks later to discuss the findings in person, I circulated around the room before the presentation began to introduce myself to the panelists. One of them said to me that he was looking forward to the presentation because he did not actually read the report. Inside my head, I thought all kinds of rude things, but out of my mouth I joked about how he must be busy, and then he said that was not the issue. He opened his copy of the report where this graph appeared in the executive summary. Here is what it looked like to him:

FIGURE 4.2   Same line graph as it appeared to a reader, having been copied and faxed

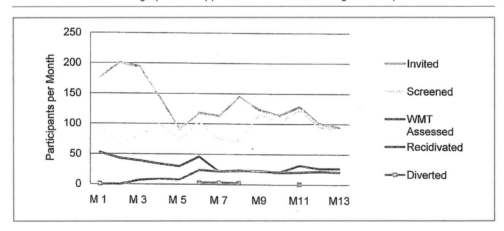

You can immediately notice that the color of the top two lines (originally blue and red) had degraded significantly, which is often the case when we distribute our work electronically and our professors or clients or supervisors print it, fax it, and then copy it for dissemination.

I learned the hard way: He was only going to look at the graphs, not read. If the visual did not pull him in, he would not proceed. All of the information in the graph was summarized in the text around it and he was not going to bother with it. Consequently, I check how my color choices look when printed in black and white. Sometimes that means I work only in grayscale. Other times, I take greater control over the distribution of my work, creating and shipping physical color copies.

Either way, I learned to be more mindful of my color choices. In this chapter, I help you to become more mindful as well.

Why Is Color Important to Memory?

Color is among the first elements that grab our earliest attention, and this fact is not just true of humans. Animals also know that color communicates; the more colorful the frog, the more poisonous. Contemporary graphic designers use color in a similar way—to draw attention to selective elements of interest (Samara, 2007). Color is one of the primary attributes of objects readily recognized by the eye-brain system. Effective data presentation uses color to quickly draw the reader's attention.

Color is not just for looking flashy, however. Viewers actually need text color to be pretty toned down in order to read it. Legibility, of course, is critical for information to be read and remembered. Such a muted setting aids legibility, but also lets chosen elements appropriately pop out when selected emphasis colors are applied. For color to stand out, the surrounding text or data points must be in a neutral color like a shade of gray. Then color can be applied, such as through color-coding systems, where colored icons correspond to colored report headings, to significantly speed navigation (Campbell & Maglio, 1999).

But, even more than legibility and efficient engagement with our data presentation, the smart use of color connects to the emotions of the viewer. Studies indicate that color is closely related to invoking and building new memories and associations that are often steeped in culture, stereotypes, and personal experience (Clarke & Costall, 2008). Thus, color choices should always be intentional.

What Colors Should I Choose?

Like most things in life, the answer to this question is the dreaded "it depends." But the fork in the decision road is actually pretty clear. It depends on the data presentation purpose. If the presentation piece at hand is intended for study and requires extensive reading of narrative prose, the color combinations should be fairly bland and nondescript. If parts of the data presentation—like a callout box of text or a key data point—need to leap out at a reader, a more colorful scheme is warranted. Let's discuss each of these in turn.

The Best Color Combinations for Reading

Guiding Idea

Narrative text is dark gray or black

Here is a bad slide I created a long time ago for a real client. I am showing you this to hurt your eyes so much that you will never forget how bad design looks (and this is just the two-color version!).

FIGURE 4.3 Generalized version of a slide with ineffective color combinations that I actually delivered to a client

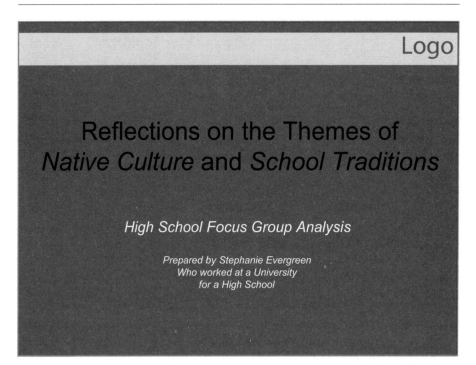

The research on color contrast says that color text on a color background hinders reading (Ware, 2013). This slide contained dark blue text on a bright blue background and these kinds of combinations make any content difficult for people to read, especially outside of a slideshow context, such as in the long passages of a report.

In a famous readability test conducted by Wheildon (2005), 53% of the study subjects did not even attempt to read the study materials when the page background color of the material was as dark as the background in Figure 4.3. For those persevering people who did continue to read, less than 50% were able to correctly answer questions on a comprehension test about the content they had just read. When color text is on color background, both legibility and comprehension are impaired. Black text has the highest comprehension levels when positioned on a white background, followed closely by dark gray text. We discuss other color options, but keep in mind that all of them come in a distant third place.

The issue is not so much about color combination as it is about contrast. The two colors must sufficiently contrast for a reader to be able to distinguish the letters from the background. Since black and white have the strongest possible contrast, some folks also like to use white (or light) on black (or very dark) backgrounds, as I did at the bottom of the worst slide I ever

> ## Guiding Idea
>
> Background has white or subdued color

created in Figure 4.3. Graphic designers refer to this color combination as "reversed out." The contrast is there. Yet it still produces weaker comprehension scores than black on white, so its use should be restricted to short bursts of text in sans serif fonts that are fairly large in size so that legibility is stable.

Studies show you can stretch the contrast without hurting legibility such that the background is no more than a 10% tint (Wheildon, 2005). It is probably fair to say that the concept of "tint" is not really a concept that most of us in report writing and graph making are familiar with (though a professional printing service knows how to handle it). Neither is it a language or concept that Microsoft speaks very well. But, for a good rule of thumb, refer to the second row of color options in Microsoft's default Office color menu.

FIGURE 4.4   This screenshot shows how to change the color of a page. The option highlighted is about as dark as you can go before hindering legibility

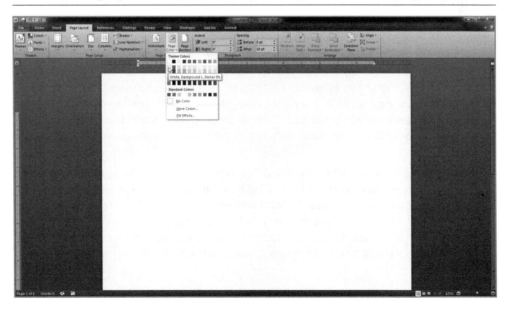

The only option shown in this example that is suitable is the choice on the left. Notice how, on hovering, it tells us that this is Darker 5%, which means a 5% tint.

Compare it to the regular white background, shown below.

FIGURE 4.5 This screenshot shows a completely white background, for comparison to the "dark" background in Figure 4.4

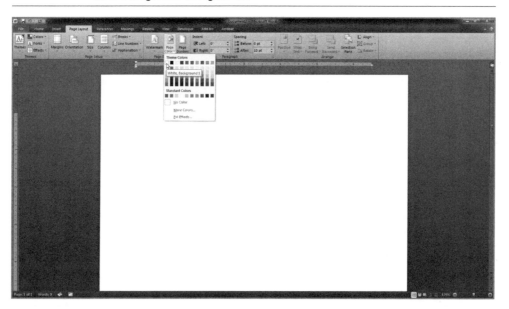

As you can see, the difference between the two backgrounds is incredibly subtle, but the slightly darker version may add some warmth to your data presentation.

The slightly darker gray just below it is a 15% tint, which is too much. The other colors in the second row, extending to the right of the ideal color, are also too dark, usually at 20% tint. If you really want to work with one of those colors, select the 20% tint option, then click on *More colors*, and scale back the slider in the *Custom color* tab to lighten it up a bit.

That said, this ad from the Ad Council and Feeding America breaks those rules and gets away with it. Here we have green color text on an orange color background. The reason it works for them is because the text is a very large sans serif, the colors are still far from each other in terms of contrast, and there is very little text to begin with. Sometimes we make choices like this for aesthetic reasons, to fit in with our university's color scheme, for example. Generally though, the best option is to use black, white, and a university color for emphasis.

FIGURE 4.6 Advertisement uses dark text on a colored background yet maintains legibility

Source: © 2012 Reprinted with permission from Feeding America.

The Best Colors for Emphasis

Although we clearly justified the predominant use of black and white, we still want some additional color because we need some method of emphasis, something that grabs early attention and lands our content in long-term memory— something effective.

Guiding Idea

One or two emphasis colors are used

Emphasis colors can be applied to headings (muted for subheadings), used for backgrounds in callout boxes where the text is short, or for calling attention to key data points in graphs.

As noted, often the emphasis colors are an easy choice, based on company or school color schemes. In my experience, organization and university color palettes often do not include enough variation in the colors—that is, there may not be a light enough color to serve as a background or a dark enough color to apply to narrative text. On many occasions, you need to completely construct your own color scheme from scratch.

Using a Color Picking Tool

Here is a procedure I use all the time to help me select color combinations for my data presentations. It makes use of an online program that incorporates all the scientific color theory stuff and then translates it for those of us without a Master of Fine Arts degree.

If I do not already have a departmental template or style sheet to work with, I first head to the organization's or client's website and take a screenshot that includes the main color scheme and then select one.

FIGURE 4.7   First, grab a screenshot from the organizational website

Then I use this cool, free program, called Adobe Kuler (pronounced "color," I'm pretty sure) at kuler.adobe.com/, which is a color picking website. Once you sign in, you can upload your selected image (in this case, the Sage screenshot). The program picks out the colors from the image.

Once I save, I can click a little slide rule icon that gives me the RGB (red/green/blue) color codes. With those color code numbers, I can customize the palette of my word-processing and presentation and graphing software programs to match the colors to those in the source image screenshot file.

FIGURE 4.8   Then upload the screenshot to Adobe Kuler

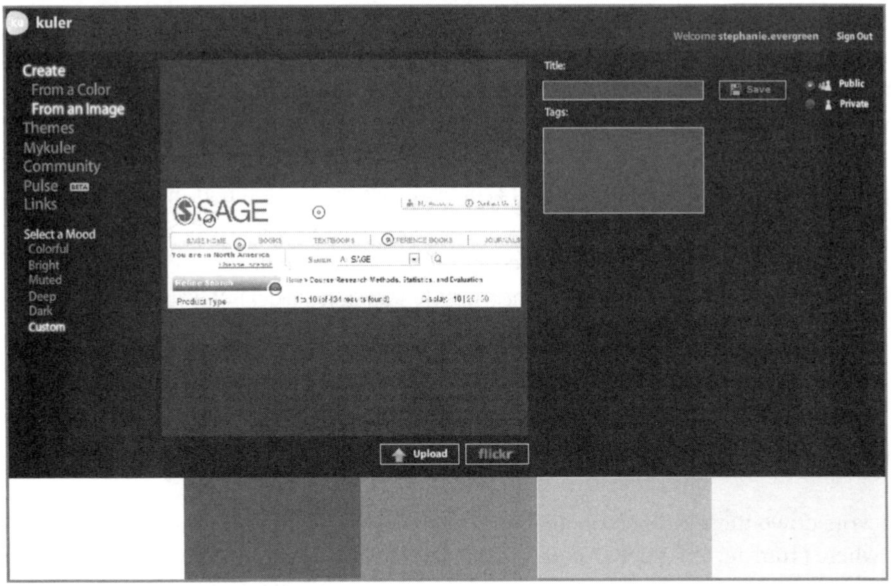

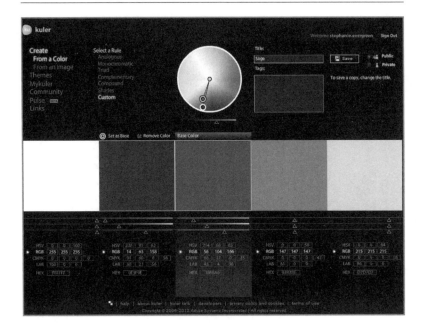

FIGURE 4.9   The program provides the color codes you need, in many forms, to customize the palette in your reporting and graphing software

Shouldn't Screen and Print Colors Match?

Chances are, if you go through this process of pulling out colors from a screenshot and adjusting your color palette in your report, when you print your report you will feel a ping of disappointment. Color rarely looks the same on paper as it does on screen, even when working with color codes. Screen monitor colors, printing ink levels, and other factors influence how well the two colors match. But, as Ware (2013) notes, precision is less important than perception. Aim to get as close as possible, without worrying about an exact match. RGB is most appropriate for things viewed on a screen. Printed materials look best with another color code, called CMYK (cyan, magenta, yellow, and black—yes, K stands for black). Both sets of color code numbers are available through most color picking tools. If you plan to print, then follow the same instructions listed here: just pop the CMYK colors into Word. However, just know that slight differences in color are such a rampant problem that it is seen as normal.

 I just write down those RGB color codes and head over to Word. Here I am showing a screenshot where I transferred the RGB codes from Kuler into the *Custom Colors* option (right-click on, say, Heading 1 in the *Styles* menu and select *Modify*, then click on the arrow by the color menu, go down to *More Colors*, and click on the *Custom* tab).

FIGURE 4.10   This screenshot shows how to navigate to the window where you can type in color codes

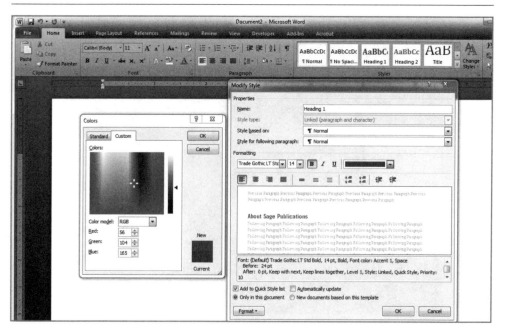

Once you set up your page layout to your preference, go to the *Themes* button and select *Save Current Theme*. Check out the instructions and screenshots in the final chapter. This process makes your color scheme available in Excel, PowerPoint, or any of the Microsoft programs.

Sometimes as I mentioned, the color scheme is not extensive enough for your purposes. In the example shown here, the three colors in the middle would not be easily distinguishable as lines in a line graph, as you can probably surmise from their rendering in grayscale for this book.

No problem. In the Kuler program, you can choose one of the colors as a "base" and then click on the optional color combination rules to generate schemes that align with color theory and play nicely with your original colors.

FIGURE 4.11 Adobe Kuler also generates alternate palettes from your selected base color

Now there are some lighter and darker options that can serve as report accents, suitable text shades, and additions to a color-coding system.

Why go to all that trouble? Because now you have created an intentional tone that communicates consistency and belonging with the work of your department or client, and that is what evaluation and research should be.

Other Color Combination Sites

If you must come up with totally original schemes, because there is no source color available, all is not lost. At this very moment, there are legions of folks just like us adding color scheme possibilities to crowd-sourced websites. Adobe Kuler has a Community section where you can peruse the contributions of others. Design Seeds at www.design-seeds.com/ and COLOURlovers at www.colourlovers.com/ are also two resources for submitted color palettes.

FIGURE 4.12   COLOURlovers has user-generated color palettes to browse. Just be mindful—not all are designed for presenting data effectively

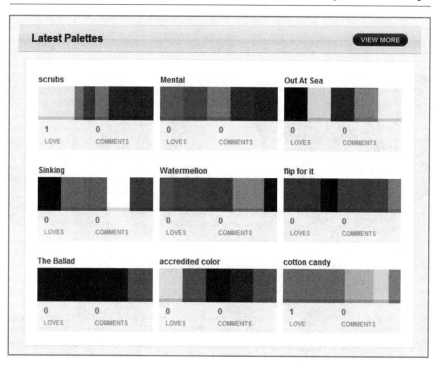

Choosing a color palette from scratch gives you the opportunity to explore how color can shape a feeling of relevancy or create a mood (Carruthers, Morris, Tarrier, & Whorwell, 2010). Even though you are reading it in gray tone, imagine the shade of pink used in the color scheme called "cotton candy." It may be difficult for some people to connect to a document using that color because of connotations related to childishness or, even more stereotypically, severe femininity. Yet it might work well in certain contexts. The color scheme called "scrubs" consists of shades of grays and blues. While some might associate that with hospitals, others might see it as the color scheme of corporate America (for better or for worse), still others might associate the colors with a rival university's football team and begin to feel some hostility. Colors definitely influence pleasure and displeasure, so it is worth running your ideas past a few classmates or colleagues to get a sense of how any color scheme you select is perceived in your localized culture.

Just keep in mind that you want a palette that includes a very dark, a very light, and at least one emphasis color. As you can see in Figure 4.12, the Ballad palette does not have enough contrast in it to suffice for data presentation purposes. There are more considerations to be mindful of when discussing color choices.

What Should I Watch Out For?

Working with color can be exciting for you and your readers. Here are three common mistakes to avoid so that color choices complement rather than compete with your data presentation efforts. Be alert to the overuse of color, colorblind readers, and reprinting in black and white.

Too Much Color

The use of color for emphasis impedes comprehension if too many colors are used indiscriminately; readers expect that a change in color indicates a change in meaning and they spend valuable time and effort trying to understand the meaning shift (Jamet, Garota, & Quaireau, 2008; Tourangeau, Couper, & Conrad, 2007).

Observe the two logic models in Figures 4.13 and 4.14, identical save for the application of color. The colorless logic model may look plain, but there is conceptually a lot going on, with arrows crossing arrows and multiple boxes in one column leading to single boxes in the next. The organizational program represented by this logic model is complicated in and of itself. The addition of color in the model in Figure 4.14 does not add clarity.

FIGURE 4.13   Basic logic model without color

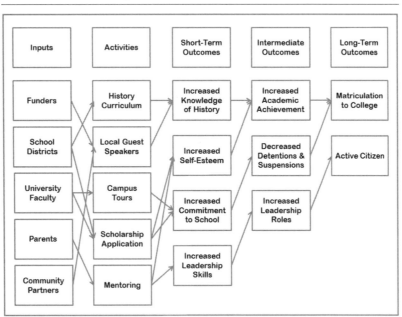

FIGURE 4.14 Same logic model, just with color

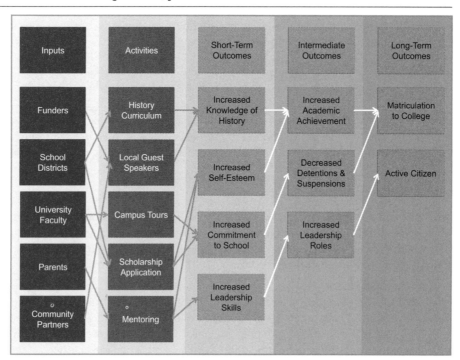

In fact, I believe that the color in the logic model in Figure 4.14 adds clutter. The color block-ing behind each column in the model is probably unnecessary, as the columns are already spaced far enough apart to distinguish them from one another. Additionally, some arrows are now white. Because of this change, readers spend time and mental capacity trying to understand if the change is meaningful. Does the nature of the program change between those levels of outcomes? No, the arrows are white simply so that they show up against the darker background. The color change is conceptually meaningless. Yet the outcomes are all assigned the same shade of blue in order to set them apart from inputs and activities—so in that area of the logic model, color is meaningful. This example quickly gets confusing; too much color gets in the way of comprehension.

Another reason to be wary of too many colors is that colors are expensive to print. The computer lab's color copies are always more expensive than the black-and-white machine for a reason. Professional printing shops significantly increase costs to run a full color, or what they call "four-color" copy job (the four colors are cyan, magenta, yellow, and K—or black—and this is the CMYK term that we discussed in the sidebar earlier). It is much less expensive to print and work with a black-and-white setting. In that case, shades of gray can accomplish a lot. Two-color printing is slightly more expensive, but not as bad as four-color. Two-color printing is usually black plus an emphasis color. Again, shades or gradations of both can actually provide a pretty wide variety of options to work with, as this book illus-trates. Most journals and publishers opt for a black-and-white or two-color scheme.

That said, don't fall into the trap of using too many shades of your emphasis color, either. Readers have a hard time distinguishing between more than four shades of a single color (Ware, 2013). So when the guiding idea states that we should have two emphasis colors (at most), include shades of one color in your count.

Colorblind Readers

Another issue to keep in mind when choosing color is colorblindness. Colorblindness on the red/green spectrum affects roughly 10% of the population in the United States. It is more common in men than in women. There are also people affected by colorblindness on the blue/yellow spectrum, though it is not as common.

Dealing with potential audience colorblindness is not as mysterious as it seems. (When taking colorblindness into account, an added bonus is that you also fortify your data presentation against the dim bulb in the projector, or the color settings on the conference room laptop that skew your established color scheme.)

Several programs are available online or downloaded to your computer to assess whether your work is accessible to those with colorblindness. Some are listed at the end of this chapter. My preference is the colorblindness simulator offered by Etre (www.etre.com/tools/colourblindsimulator/). The simulator renders your files into how they appear to people with various colorblindness conditions.

With the following example (be prepared to cringe), I used another program called Vischeck (www.vischeck.com/), on a slide I developed to look like others I have seen. My slide is on the left. It is green text with a red background. The slide on the right shows what it look likes if you are affected by red-green colorblindness (the condition is known as deuteranopia).

FIGURE 4.15   Vischeck shows how the image appears under certain variations of colorblindness

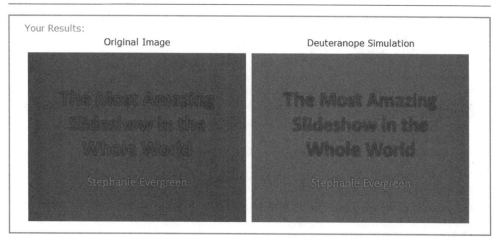

True, the image is terrible, but the original image on the left is pretty bad in the first place! So, the problem is not really about the red-green color combination—it is about the contrast of the two colors. Below, I still used red and green to make my original slide, but note the improved readability, both before and after Vischeck:

FIGURE 4.16   A stronger contrast between colors used on text and background boosts legibility, even under colorblindness or black-and-white printing

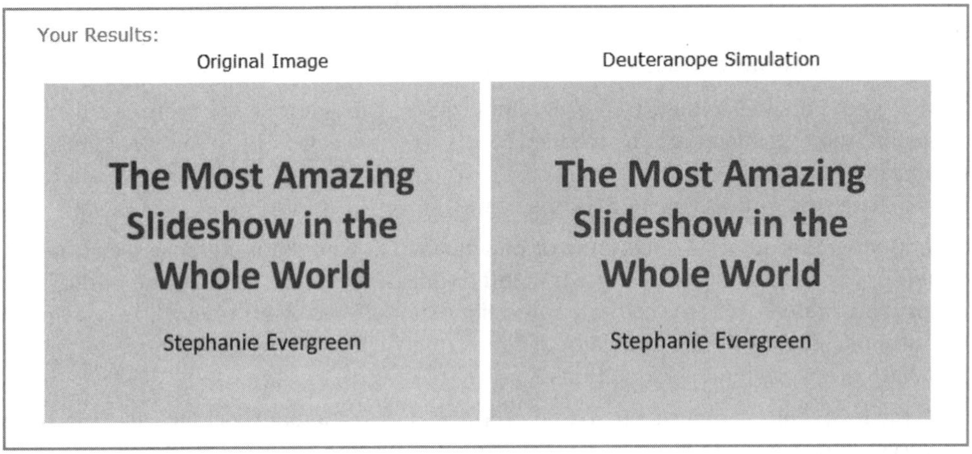

Your Results:

Original Image

Deuteranope Simulation

The Most Amazing Slideshow in the Whole World

Stephanie Evergreen

The Most Amazing Slideshow in the Whole World

Stephanie Evergreen

The message is to not be afraid of color combinations—but do focus on making certain that you have a light-dark color pairing that is maintained regardless of the projector quality, presentation laptop color settings, or audience impairment.

For RGB color schemes that are appropriate for those with colorblindness, check out ColorBrewer 2.0 at www.colorbrewer2.com/. This is a free web program that lets you select the number of colors you need and the nature of your data (sequential or diverging, for example) and then produces color palettes that are colorblind-safe. Originally intended for cartography, you can go through the steps to obtain effective color codes that are applicable to any sort of data presentation.

Does Color Apply Universally?

When choosing a good emphasis color, always keep in mind the possible cultural connotations it may carry and how those connotations vary globally. The field of color psychology investigates what associations different cultures bring to the same color. Blue, for example, is commonly associated with liberal politics in the United States. In the United Kingdom, it represents conservatives. Baby blue is often associated with boys in the United States, while in China some presume blue is a feminine color. It also can represent authority; conversely, it can mean depression. Blue is often believed to be one of the safest colors to use worldwide, nevertheless, it still communicates different cultural messages based on the shade and the context. Other colors are even less universal; therefore, the context of your dissemination should influence your color choices.

Reprinting in Black and White

Similar to the way the lines in my graph deteriorated under the normal wear-and-tear of research dissemination, always check that your intentional color choices and emphasis are stable after normal transmission methods.

Guiding Idea

Color reprints legibly in black and white

In this sample report page, the original in Figure 4.17 uses only grayscale. There are a few leader words at the start of the main paragraphs that are in a dark gray. In the graph, the darkest color—black—is used to emphasize the graduation rate. I copied that page, faxed it, and copied it again to replicate a normal dissemination route. The result is Figure 4.18.

FIGURE 4.17   The original page

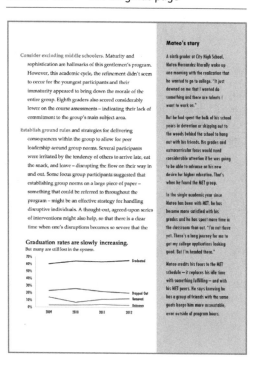

FIGURE 4.18 The result, after normal wear and tear, shows some degradation to the intentional use of color in the graph

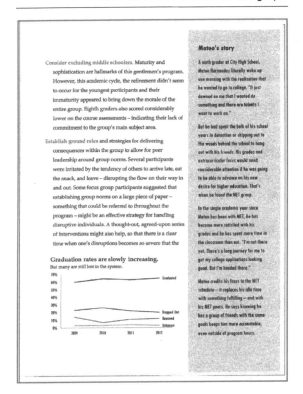

While the content generally held up all right, we can see that the leader text disintegrated somewhat, making it harder to read. The black graduation line in the graph at the bottom faded considerably, diminishing its emphasis. And the background of the sidebar is distractingly grainy, impacting legibility.

To check legibility, print using your printer's grayscale settings, then make a black-and-white copy of that printout (and then maybe a copy of that copy), or fax it to yourself. In this case rather than change the leader text to a dark gray, I could have kept it black and bolded it. I also could have created greater difference between the shades of color in the lines of the graph.

How Do I Apply Emphasis Colors?

Now that we have taken the care to develop an intentional color scheme, let's look at effective ways to use those colors in our data presentations. Usually color serves one of two purposes:

1. Decorating
2. Spotlighting

Decorating

It may sound as if this reason to use color is superfluous, not for those interested in seriously effective data presentation. However, applying colors for decoration adds a balance and professionalism to reports that contribute to perceptions of credibility and quality.

FIGURE 4.19   Report cover where text color and text background color have been pulled from main image

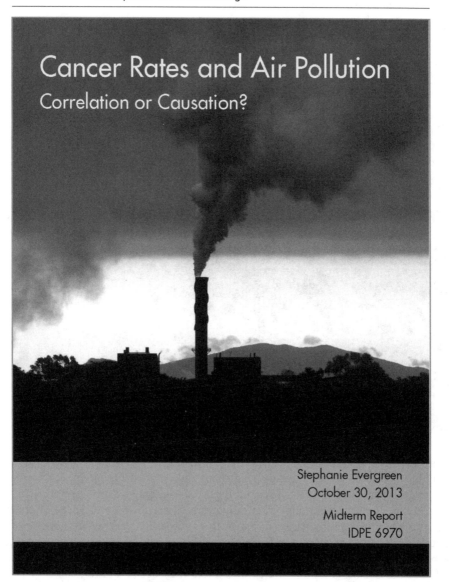

In this midterm report cover, a large photograph of a factory smokestack consumes the page. Go online to this book's website (www.sagepub.com/evergreen) to see this image in color and then keep reading. The photograph is cast in shades of blue and gray. The author's information is listed at the bottom of the report cover, placed against a blue strip of color—the same blue that appears in the photograph. Even the light gray-blue used on the title text comes directly from the photograph. The repetition of color adds a cohesiveness that communicates forethought and planning—just what we want to express as a student. You can readily replicate this look by using any of the color picking tools in this chapter to pull out the exact color from the photograph and then customize the fill color of a text box in Word.

FIGURE 4.20   Slide uses a limited color palette to convey the key message of influence

This slide shows another use of color as a decorative tool. The background on the left is a dark blue and the text shifts from dark gray to very light gray as it progresses down the slide. We know this sort of situation can impact legibility. The gray on the word "Design" is too dark and the blue background is technically unnecessary. However, the use of color here suggests a change. The progression of grayscale is used to reflect the way good design can change a reader's mind. There is a purpose to the decoration, an intentional color selection. The background on the right, behind the image, even matches the very light gray on the word "Persuasion." So although the color choices may not be entirely ideal by legibility standards, they work well to express a concept and they fit together as a united package. Furthermore, this example illustrates the effective decorative use of color even when full-color printing is not an option.

Spotlighting

The second important use of color (and the one we spend the most time on throughout this chapter), is applying an emphasis color to bring attention to your data.

FIGURE 4.21   Repeating the title text box's background color on the callout text box background helps to spotlight the key takeaway message

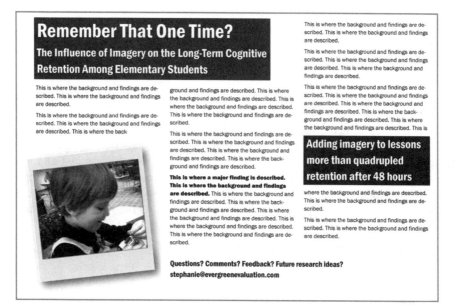

While we know light text on a dark background is less than perfect, it is still effective in drawing attention to short bits of text. The callout box on this poster does just that. The fill color of the callout box is a dark gray to draw the eye, emphasizing the study's main finding. Then, I changed the text box fill color behind the title in order to add balance to the poster. If the heaviness of the dark text box was only applied to the callout on the right, the poster looks a bit odd or lopsided. Although I elected to use dark gray here to achieve this look, other appropriately dark emphasis color choices also work.

Further, I added bolding to two sentences in the middle of the narrative text. In essence, this made them blacker. As a general rule of thumb, it is best to keep the narrative text uniform, but note that sometimes a color change (even bolding) can call a reader's attention as well. As usual, we would not want to overuse this color emphasis technique.

FIGURE 4.22 A callout box or a slide can use color on the important statistic to help it draw reader attention and memory

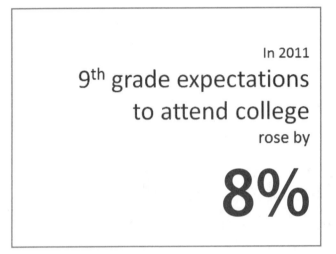

In 2011

9th grade expectations to attend college

rose by

8%

You can also use color to call attention to an important sidebar or statistic. Here, the figure illustrates the very selective use of color to make the 8% pop out. Note how the rest of the text must be in dark gray rather than black. Black and white is the strongest contrast, so anytime we use color to emphasize text, we actually weaken the contrast and make the important text stand out less. Ironic, right? This problem is not always noticeable—it depends a great deal on the emphasis color in question. The lighter the emphasis color, the less it actually stands out when applied. However, by making the rest of the narrative dark gray, the color text pops out even more.

Now we turn to using color for emphasis in data visualizations.

How Do I Apply These Ideas to Graphs?

We are going to start by talking about how Excel, as great as it is, has color default settings that for several reasons are not preferable. Let's talk about color in terms of background, legend, data points, and even how it looks across multiple graphs.

Guiding Idea

Background has white/ subdued color

Background Color

To begin, backgrounds should be white. Some default chart templates in Excel and other programs apply a gray color to the background that makes it even harder for the colors of the data points to contrast and maintain legibility. The APA Guide asks that shading should be limited and distinct (p. 161); therefore, it is best to reserve the use of color for the data, not the background.

Color Discrimination in Legends

In his 2010 book, *Designing with the Mind in Mind,* Jeff Johnson talks about charts, their legends, and color discrimination. Jeff points out how it is hard for people to distinguish legend colors when rendered in Excel's default mode. With a few added cleanup modifications, Figure 4.23 is what the typical chart looks like in Excel.

You can see that when the default Excel colors are reprinted in black and white (as is commonly the case with my budget-conscious peers, clients, and journal editors), it is hard to match up which line associates with which label.

FIGURE 4.23 A line graph produced with default Excel colors does not hold up well in black and white

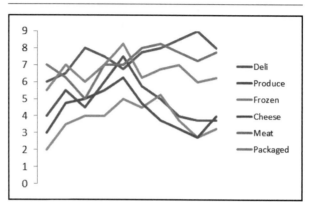

But, even in the full-color variation (which you can view online) Johnson notes that the small sizes of the legend entries cause color discrimination problems, particularly among shades of blue.

We discuss other options later; however let's say for now, we are committed to the default Excel colors. How can we improve color discrimination? In those cases, we can listen to Jeff's recommendation to enlarge the legend entries so that they are more identifiable and distinguishable.

But you cannot really change the size of the legend entries in Excel. So, I improvised by inserting a rectangle, matching the color, and placing it right over the label in the legend.

For those situations where a legend is still critical, the increased size of the label entries eases the interpretability of the graph. Nevertheless, I bet it is still pretty hard for you to view this in black and white and discern the colors in the bars. Thank goodness that I am going to show you other options.

Single Emphasis Color on Data Points

Working with that default color scheme may be appropriate when you are analyzing the data. When you are in your office looking for patterns or abnormalities, it can be helpful to distinguish each line or

FIGURE 4.24 Larger areas of color in the legend aid color discrimination

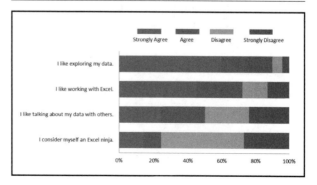

data point by marking it with a different color. But when reporting and presenting this data, research shows this causes confusion. Color changes signal a change in the hierarchy of the information; however in spite of this, designers often do not have any kind of hierarchy in mind—the color is just to be pretty. Numerous scholars suggest that the rainbow use impedes comprehension of the data (Few, 2006; So & Smith, 2002; Tufte, 2001).

Guiding Idea

Color changes denote meaning changes

A grayscale palate plus one emphasis color is a much more understandable option. In Figure 4.25, I deemphasized the less important data by switching the colors of those lines to shades of gray and I used my highlight color to support the communication of my message, which is then reiterated in the chart title area.

FIGURE 4.25   Highlighting important information with a single emphasis color makes the graph's takeaway message more obvious

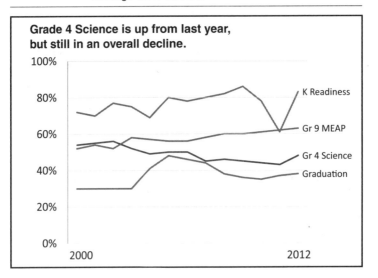

When using a grayscale plus emphasis color palette, keep in mind that the gray should still be fairly dark. As the APA Guide (2010) notes, data should be darker than the gridlines, just as shown in Figure 4.25.

Guiding Idea

One or two emphasis colors are used

In Figure 4.26 you see the smart use of color in a bar graph. No question about what I want you to notice, is there? My main category of interest is the Michigan bar, so I applied my project's chosen blue color to bring attention to it. In this particular example, I also added a red vertical line, to indicate a predetermined score cut point or goal.

Color can also be used in other types of data displays, such as in a table.

In Figure 4.27, I use color to show areas of survey responses in need of attention. I simply change the cell border color from No Color to my emphasis color. It is shown in blue here, but when I made this table for a real client, I was working with the red/yellow/green color scheme strongly associated with traffic lights in the United States. In hindsight, I probably should have used other colors in order to address potential colorblindness issues. Darker colors contrast with the background more, so, to display the table now, I chose a color gradation system where a darker blue marks cells requesting the most attention and a medium blue surrounds data requiring only moderate attention.

Whatever you choose, the key is to use the emphasis colors consistently, as we talk about next.

Color-Coding Data Across Multiple Graphs

The gray plus one color scheme works well for many situations. However, sometimes that palette is too restrictive for data presentation and a stronger impact can be made by assigning particular colors to certain pieces of data. Like how we all know green means go, color-coding data eases interpretability.

Let's imagine that I want to report the responses to some survey questions,

FIGURE 4.26   By using an emphasis color on the bar for Michigan, I highlight that data for the reader

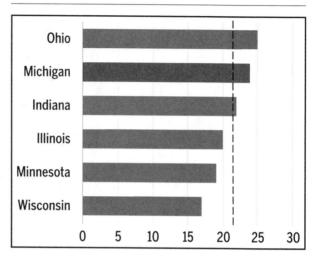

FIGURE 4.27   Cell borders can be changed to the emphasis color to highlight particular figures

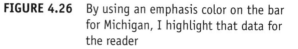

9th Grade College Expectations

	Strongly Disagree	Disagree	Neutral	Agree	Strongly Agree
I expect to go to college	1.5%	5.4%	5.2%	31.2%	56.7%
My parents expect me to go to college	8.2%	7.7%	14.9%	46.3%	22.9%
My teachers expect me to go to college	1.8%	24.7%	28.3%	31.1%	14.1%

and the response options are on a standard Likert-type scale. In this scenario, I like my readers to generally group the positive and negative responses into one mental chunk—in other words, the Strongly Agree responses and Agree responses conceptually group together, as do the Strongly Disagree and Disagree. But I also want to show the responses for each category,

FIGURE 4.28   Divergent color schemes can visually group similar survey responses

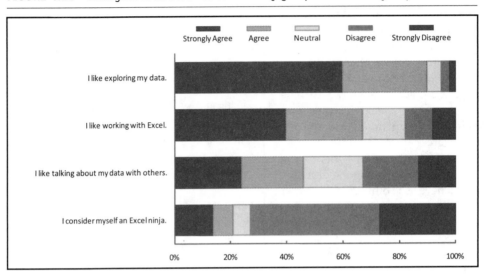

because of the need to pay attention to those who marked Agree and Disagree in order to focus on tipping them one way or the other. It's important that these responses are distinct.

This is the type of research condition where a diverging color scheme comes in very handy. The positive responses here are in shades of blue—with the stronger response in the darker shade. The negative responses here are in shades of gray. Shading within one color identifies those data points as a group but also lets them maintain some distinguishability from one another. Then, throughout my narrative, I use blue and gray to reinforce the color coding and increase engagement with the data presentation. With separate graphs solely focused on the negative responses, the data points are in a gray palette. If I have a callout box in my narrative that captures a positive comment, the background of the box is blue. Clarity is achieved through the color choices.

How Can I Handle Light on White?

In the same Figure 4.28, the neutral category is set in a very light blue-gray. Generally speaking, light colors on a white background are the worst color combinations for legibility. The light colors do not contrast well with white. Yet, in this diverging color scheme, it is important to have a neutral shade in between the blue and gray poles. Instead of adjusting the light color, I added a thin, slightly darker border around the neutral colored data point in the stacked bar to help set that color off from the white background.

Alternatively, if the data display is being shown to an audience with the explicit hope that they compare data points, assigning scales within one color can speed interpretation and increase accuracy (Brewslow, Ratwani, & Trafton, 2009). This idea of using gradations of one color also helps with the interpretation of line graphs when the lines cross one another substantially, or of scatterplots where the chart area holds different categories of data.

In this figure, a gradated color scheme makes sense as applied to an ordinal scale of high school grades. The higher the grade, the darker the color. We even reinforced the color scheme by making the data labels at the end of each line the matching color. And notice how much easier it is to distinguish among the lines where they cluster and intertwine on the left of the graph. For example, this color system can be incorporated throughout the rest of the report, where the headings that pertain to 9th graders are always set in the lightest blue of the palette, which is still dark enough to be legible on heading text. When we put grade-level data in tables, we use the same colors on the column headers. Color-coding systems build an interpretive, systematic structure that is supportive of the viewer's efforts to engage with our data.

Eventually, we refine the color use so that more complex data, such as in this scatterplot does not even need a legend cluttering it up in order to understand what each color signifies.

Consistent use of the color system results in faster interpretation and easier engagement. Keep in mind, however, that it is difficult for readers to detect differences when more than four shades are used.

Once a color code is assigned to each category, it should not change. The color assignment is listed in the project's design plan or style sheet (see Chapter 6) and unwaveringly followed. When the color scheme shifts, the audience gets confused and exerts precious mental energy and attention trying to decipher the meaning behind the color shift.

In Figures 4.31 and 4.32, the direction of the color progression reverses between graphs. Even more, the lightest blue color in each graph (Strongly Disagree for Classroom A and Strongly Agree for Classroom B) is actually two

FIGURE 4.29   Color gradations applied to ordinal categories can also visually organize data

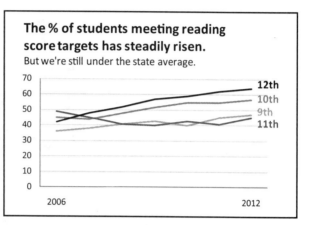

FIGURE 4.30   Introducing a consistent color-coding system can bring understanding to a graph without the use of a legend or labels

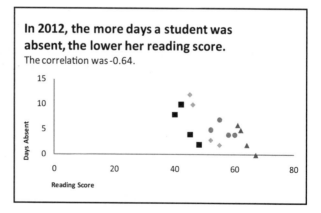

FIGURE 4.31 This chart may appear in one part of a report . . .

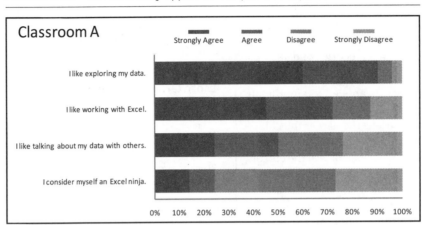

FIGURE 4.32 . . . while this chart appears in another. Inconsistent color-coding throughout a single report leads to confusion

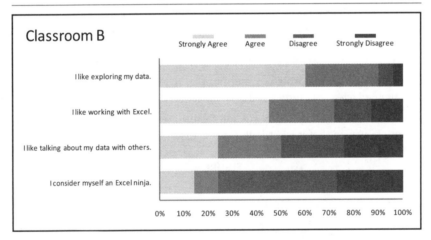

different shades, which could spur a careful reader to wonder what the difference between the two light blue colors represents. This confusion persists, even when the graphs are separated by pages of narrative or explanatory slides. So, decide on a color-coding system and stick with it. Once established, the color-coding system works to assist your presentation in powerful ways.

Color-coding operates at peak efficiency levels when used on data dashboards. We have not discussed dashboards very much; basically, they are an amalgamation of the individual data visualizations we have been talking about. Dashboards quickly summarize key information, usually a handful of the most important indicators for a program or organization. It is an information-packed, clean one-page handout that serves as a nice launching pad when sharing your data with stakeholders and funders, or high-level supervisors and vice presidents—it is their overview of what's happening, from 30,000 feet.

FIGURE 4.33   This dashboard relies on a color-coding system introduced in the top row, which keeps the bottom row uncluttered

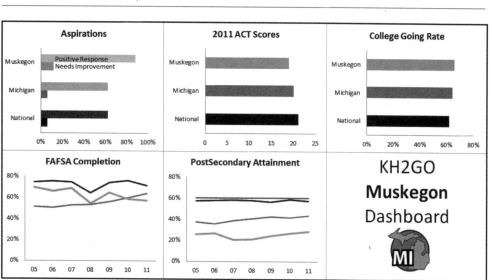

Source: © 2011 Reprinted with permission from the American Council on Education. KnowHow2GO is a registered trademark used with permission from the American Council on Education.

This sample dashboard works with a fairly restricted project color scheme I developed—just orange, gray, black, and a tiny hint of blue (in the background of the circle behind the shape of Michigan). Notice how we built a color system where, in most of the graphs, the city is in the emphasis orange color, Michigan is gray, and the National scores are black. Then, when we get down to the line graphs in the second row, I can even get away with having no labels at all, because the interpretive system is now established. The only place this system requires extra elaboration is the very first graph in the upper left, where each location had some subcategories that needed labeling. In these areas, I used lighter shades of each assigned color.

The color-coding system supports the primary purpose of dashboards—to provide rapid and easy engagement and interpretation for our audience so that we can quickly move into informed discussion and decision making.

What Is the Bottom Line?

Selective use of color is one way the designer (you) can "prechunk" your information, easing some of the thinking and cogitating a reader normally has to do, thus increasing both their capacity of thinking and the amount of time an audience spends thinking about your data. The effective application of emphasis colors absolutely hinges on two things. First, identify the key message you are trying to communicate in your diagram, graph, or slide in order to emphasize that message with color. Second, once you set up a palette of colors, use those color choices consistently to create a predictable system for your readers that speeds up their ability to understand and remember your effective data presentations.

KEY POINTS TO REMEMBER

- RGB color codes are intended for things you want to print. CMYK color codes are best suited for things that appear on screen. You can translate between the two closely, but if they do not match with exactitude, don't stress out.

- Dark gray or black should always be applied to text intended for long, narrative reading. Shorter bursts of text or those less essential to comprehension can be set in different colors or can appear on a colored background.

- The default color scheme of Excel is almost never a good idea. Apply color intentionally to specific areas of the graph to communicate a point or highlight an area for greater focus.

- Color choices degrade in black-and-white print settings and regular dissemination routes. Replicate a typical distribution of your report by copying and faxing and so on to determine whether your color scheme holds up well.

HOW CAN I EXTEND THIS?

Check Out

Adobe Kuler (http://kuler.adobe.com)—This is the color picking site shared earlier in this chapter. Upload your own photos here to pull out colors; type in one color code you have on hand to generate a full palette; or browse the color schemes invented by others.

MulticolorEngine (http://labs.tineye.com/multicolr)—Produced by the folks at TinEye Labs, this search engine lets the user locate images from Flickr based on their color. Type in the color codes you have (it only works with web codes) and the search engine produces an amazing generation of graphics containing those colors.

As I was writing this chapter, Adobe pulled its Kuler program for maintenance without any forewarning. Several friends and colleagues wrote me desperate pleas for additional resources for well-designed color schemes. Check out both COLOURlovers at http://www .colourlovers.com/ and Design Seeds at http://www.design-seeds.com/ as alternatives. But take note—Design Seeds only provides the color codes in Hex, or web-based color codes. To translate them into RGB or CMYK, use the color code converter listed next.

Color Code Converter (http://easycalculation.com/colorconverter/colorconverter.php)—If you have RGB codes and need to know how to translate those to CMYK or web codes, this is your spot. Type in what you have, click, and generate what you need.

ColorBrewer 2.0 (http://colorbrewer2.com/)—This site is designed to provide color advice for maps, but you can use the settings to produce color codes for palettes that are both colorblind-safe and printer-friendly.

Try This

Download Colorblind Assistant at http://www.achronism.com/indexadv.php#Software, a free, lightweight tool that allows you to hover on colors to reveal their color codes. Then go snag your school or organization's RGB colors.

Download Color Oracle at http://colororacle.org/index.html, right to your computer—it runs through your selected documents and shows you what they look like under the various types of colorblindness.

Test out some color palette ideas by scribbling with Crayola crayons, keeping in mind the need for a light, a dark, and an emphasis color (or two). Then go look up the web and RGB codes on Wikipedia at http://en.wikipedia.org/wiki/List_of_Crayola_crayon_colors to replicate that color scheme in your data presentations.

Snag the PicturePalette app from iTunes at http://itunes.apple.com/us/app/picturepalette/id527095741?mt=8. With this app, you can snap a photo of your favorite place, or the school you are studying, or the subject you are interviewing, and tap one color from the photo. Using that color, the app creates several color schemes and provides you with the web codes. With both the picture and the color palette, you are on your way to a cohesive design for your data presentation.

WHERE CAN I GO FOR MORE INFORMATION?

Brewslow, L. A., Ratwani, R. M., & Trafton, J. G. (2009). Cognitive models of the influence of color scale on data visualization tasks. *Human Factors, 51*(3), 321–338.

Campbell, C. S., & Maglio, P. P. (1999). Facilitating navigation in information spaces: Road-signs on the World Wide Web. *International Journal of Human-Computer Studies, 50,* 309–327.

Carruthers, H. R., Morris, J., Tarrier, N., & Whorwell, P. J. (2010). The Manchester Color Wheel: Development of a novel way of identifying color choice and its validation in healthy, anxious, and depressed individuals. *BMC Medical Research Methodology, 10*(12). Retrieved from http://www.biomedcentral.com/content/pdf/1471–2288–10–12.pdf

Clarke, T., & Costall, A. (2008). The emotional connotations of color: A qualitative investigation. *Color Research and Application, 33*(5), 406–410.

Few, S. (2006). *Information dashboard design.* Sebastopol, CA: O'Reilly.

Jamet, E., Garota, M., & Quaireau, C. (2008). Attention guiding in multimedia learning. *Learning and Instruction, 18,* 135–145.

Johnson, J. (2010). *Designing with the mind in mind.* Burlington, MA: Morgan Kaufmann.

Samara, T. (2007). *Design elements: A graphic style manual.* Beverly, MA: Rockport Press.

So, S., & Smith, M. (2002). Colour graphics and task complexity in multivariate decision making. *Accounting, Auditing & Accountability Journal, 15*(4), 565–593.

Tourangeau, R., Couper, M. P., & Conrad, F. (2007). Color, labels, and interpretive heuristics for response scales. *Public Opinion Quarterly, 71*(1), 91–112.

Tufte, E. R. (2001). *The visual display of quantitative information* (2nd ed.). Cheshire, CT: Graphics Press.

Ware, C. (2013). *Information visualization: Perception for design* (3rd ed.). Waltham, MA: Morgan Kaufmann.

Wheildon, C. (2005). *Type and layout: Are you communicating or just making pretty shapes?* Mentone, Australia: The Worsley Press.

CHAPTER 5

Arrangement

Learning Objectives

After reading this chapter you will be able to:

- Choose the proper text justification settings so that your research is easier to read
- Arrange text, graphics, and callout points to maximize impact
- Position graphics consistently
- Ease cognitive overload by grouping data with text
- Produce clearer data displays

W hen someone asks me how effective data presentation actually contributes to a better bottom line, I tell them this story.

Some time ago, I sat in a meeting with 11 other people. We were reviewing research findings, presented via graphs that were created by another researcher who was not present. You know this scene. You have been there a hundred times. The group spent 20 minutes just trying to decode and interpret a single graph. It was not the data that was confusing. It was not the graph type, either. But it was the little things like the placement of the labels that confused the 11 of us (an educated group, I should point out) and led to a lengthy graph deconstruction discussion. So, what did that weak design cost?

Guiding Ideas

Important elements are prominent

Lines of narrative text are 8 to 12 words in length

Narrative text is left or full justified

Alignment is consistent

Grouped items logically belong together

Empty area is allocated

Six people at that meeting were paid $800/day, which means we spent $200 on their confusion:

1 person at $600/day = $25

1 person at $400/day = $17

1 person at $300/day = $13

2 people at $1,500/day = $125

That one poor graph design cost our group $380, which was actually more than the daily rate (salary and benefits) for one of the meeting attendees. If the cost of living is higher in your town, or you work in a more profitable sector, then raise this amount accordingly.

Ouch. Additionally, this does not include the time it took for the report author to develop the weak graph in the first place, or the subsequent time to make the graph clearer. As common as this situation seems, it is even more costly when weak graphs are published in textbooks, magazines, or newspapers and adding in the cost of printing and reprinting and confusion on a larger scale. Bad design is expensive. Thus, an upfront time investment in learning about good design principles and applying them to data displays and presentation literally pays off in the end. The arrangement of the data tends to be the least obvious aspect of effective data presentation, so let's turn now to discuss what to do with all of those bits and pieces of information.

Where Do the Bits and Pieces Go?

The bits and pieces referenced here are the graphics, images, and blocks of text that comprise your presentation documents. Thus far, we talked about what we know we need to have—compelling images, intelligent colors, and intentional typefaces. In this chapter, we focus on how to arrange those elements on a page, slide, poster, and data display so that they support reader cognition.

Basically, we want the most important information on the page or slide to go where it dominates attention. It naturally follows then that in order to arrange the pieces in a document, the author must make decisions about what aspects of the data presentation are most important, second in importance, and so on. Just as we talked about in Chapter 3, they are essentially creating a hierarchy for the prominence of the data.

In general, it is easiest to create a hierarchy of information when the reporting format is limited to just one idea or image per page or slide, thus avoiding competition between report pieces. Once the hierarchy is established conceptually, the information is ready for arrangement in the actual software. Effective arrangement organizes presentations to support comprehension and readability. This may be one of the most advanced steps you can take as a research presentation designer, so hang on.

Guiding Idea

Important elements are prominent

Two Models for Arranging Presentation Pieces

I am about to introduce two options for arranging report pieces, but first we must predicate that work with a quick discussion of grids. When I suggested the idea of writing about grids to the graphic designers on my dissertation panel, half of them advised that I avoid this idea, explaining that grids are complicated concepts that are troublesome even for some professional graphic designers. I eschewed their suggestions because we are, after all, researchers—we love systematic organization, and that's what a grid does. You will be good at this, if you follow my lead

Essentially, grids divide a page into columns and rows so that designers have a consistent and predictable placement for each reporting element (Mueller-Brockmann, 1981). Let's come review the Greenpeace report I introduced in Chapter 2, because they did such a nice job of organizing their information.

You can download this entire report at www.greenpeace.org/international/Global/international/publications/climate/2010/fullreport.pdf.

FIGURE 5.1   Black lines mark the grid—the rows and columns used by the designer to arrange the report pieces

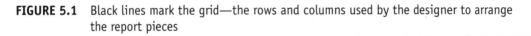

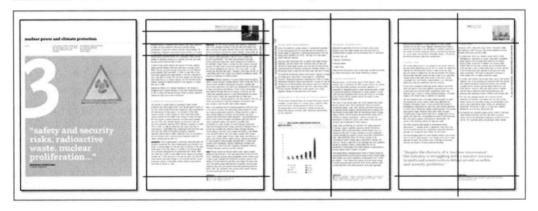

Source: © 2010 Reprinted with permission from One Hemisphere/Greenpeace.

Here, it appears that Greenpeace chose a grid that divides the pages into lots of short rows. I drew in the first three on the second page to give you a sense of the grid structure. If we extend the second line over to the left so that it stretched across the first page of this report section (get a pencil and try it), you can see that it is exactly where the thin line under the title is placed. If we stretch that second line across the more text-heavy pages to the right, the tops of the text columns begin at that same gridline. The third gridline down on the second page, extended to the left, marks the top of the box on the first page. The bits and pieces line up according to these rows.

Vertically, I detected at least two columns, again allowing for text or graphics to consume more than one column. Notice that if we copy that single vertical gridline down the middle of page 3 onto the section cover, one of the short bursts of texts under the title and to the left of the triangle graphic aligns to it. The basic structure allows for a systematic way to lay out the information throughout the report.

You can probably see other gridlines, both horizontal and vertical that I did not draw but that signal the organization of the report.

As the research report designer, using a grid structure means that I rarely have to spend time with alignment or decisions about where to place the picture on the page, because the arrangement is dictated by the grid. And as a reader, I realize that whenever I see a photo that takes up three-fourths of the rows, it is the start of a new section of the report. That sort of organization speeds navigation and increases information retention in an audience. Grid systems take out the guesswork and produce a more organized report.

To establish a grid structure, choose the number of rows and columns you like and space them evenly along a page. Use the ruler along the top and side of your software program and make note of where the gridlines fall. On an 8.5" × 11" paper, if I wanted four rows, I would want to divide 11 by 4. But, wait a minute. The rows would look more even if I took the margins into consideration. So subtracting the 1" margins from the top and bottom leaves me with 9 inches of working room. I divide 9 by 4 to see that my rows will each be 2.25" tall. Later, this helps position the graphics.

Position within the grid is important to attraction and comprehension. Viewers pay more attention to elements that compose key positions. Information lower in the hierarchy is toned down and placed in subordinate positions. Here are two models for placing elements within a grid.

Gutenberg Diagram Arrangement Model

The Gutenberg Diagram is based on research specific to Western cultures identifying the way eyes travel around a page when people engage with a document.

Some studies show that deviation from this diagram throws off comprehension of the material (Wheildon, 2005). Imagine you have all of the content you need to create a research poster about your dissertation. You sit down at your computer, open your poster software, and stare at a blank screen. According to the Gutenberg Diagram, you want to place your elements according to what people naturally look at first.

FIGURE 5.2 The Gutenberg Diagram signals where to place (and not place) key presentation pieces

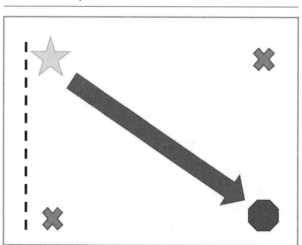

The first area on a page where a person's eyes tend to go is represented here by the star. This is known as the *primary optical area,* the most ideal spot to grab attention. In Western culture, the top left area is a key position.

The arrow represents the direction eyes flow through the material (reminder: this represents reading in Western cultures). People are most comfortable reading according to this *reading gravity*—left to right and top to bottom. Layouts that go against this reading gravity tend to make a reader feel subtly uncomfortable, which sometimes can work to the designer's advantage. (I explain more about this element later on in the chapter.)

The dotted line marks the *axis of orientation,* where eyes want to return after reading each line. Readers want a strong and predictable axis of orientation, probably at one of your gridlines. A bit further into this chapter we talk about alignment and justification of text in more detail, but the basic idea is that the narrative text should align.

The stop sign signals the *terminal area.* It is the last place eyes tend to go before leaving a page, even if the reader is just skimming.

The *fallow areas* are represented by the location of the *x*'s. Usually, these corners are left blank, or fallow. Placing standalone elements in those areas put demands on the eyes to work against reading gravity. Sometimes, continuous narrative text can run through the fallow corners and sometimes those corners can be activated with eye-catching graphics.

The Gutenberg Diagram applies more to text-heavy data presentations, such as posters and reports.

How well does the Gutenberg Diagram hold up? Pretty well.

FIGURE 5.3 Laying the Gutenberg Diagram over a poster confirms an engaging design

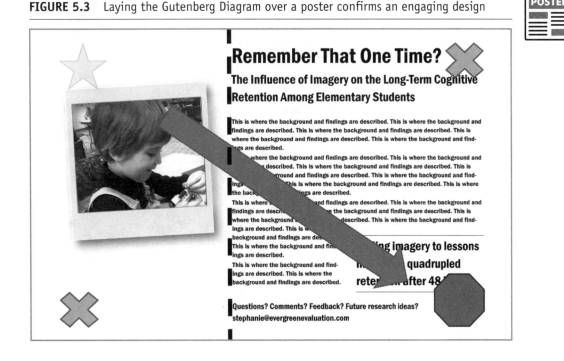

In answer to that question, this poster from Chapter 2 closely fits the model. The picture of the child is roughly in the primary optical area. The main text, including title, narrative, and contact information, aligns on a strong axis of orientation. The arrow confirms that, from the boy's face through to the last question in the lower left, the poster follows reading gravity. The end of the callout text is in the terminal area. And the fallow areas are empty.

FIGURE 5.4   The advertisement arrangement aligns with the Gutenberg Diagram

Source: © 2012. Reprinted with permission from the Coalition to End Childhood Lead Poisoning.

Figure 5.4 is an advertisement from the Ad Council. I saw this on a billboard near my house and loved it because of how well this ad catches the eye with its novelty. Now, you are not in the business of designing billboards, but think how revolutionary it would be if our research report covers and posters looked like this.

Again, how well does the ad follow the Gutenberg Diagram? The paint can is located in the primary optical area. The arrow shows that the whole ad generally moves according to reading gravity. The axis of orientation is roughly in the middle of the page but still clearly evident. Organizational logos are placed in the terminal area, the last place our eyes will go, so as to leave a lasting impression. And the fallow corners are generally left blank, except perhaps for the intriguing cereal bowl.

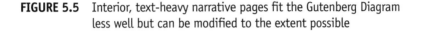

FIGURE 5.5   Interior, text-heavy narrative pages fit the Gutenberg Diagram less well but can be modified to the extent possible

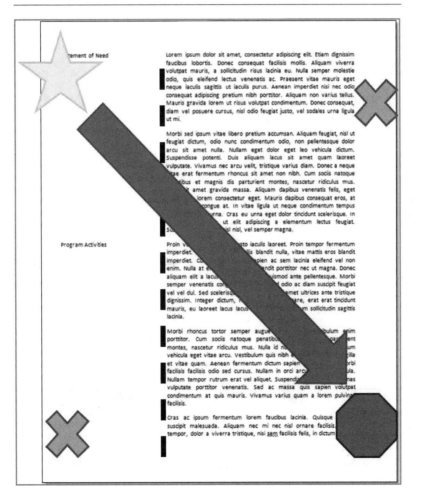

In Figure 5.5, let's look at the interior page of a report. The primary optical area is somewhat weakened with interior pages, but in this case the heading there is stuck way out to the left. This arrangement is effective organization for a report. It makes locating information a faster process for the reader, particularly when a grid structure is used to ensure the placement falls in the same location when starting a fresh page. The axis of orientation is further into the page, just as in the paint can ad, but still follows a very strong line to return to when reading, and adheres to a grid. The narrative text follows reading gravity. The terminal area is also less strong on an interior page, because the intent is that there is more reading continued on the next page. The lower left fallow area is left blank, but the upper right fallow area is activated by being filled with continuous narrative text.

Rule of Thirds Arrangement Model

Besides the Gutenberg Diagram, another common model for layout is the Rule of Thirds, which stems from photography.

Watch a short tutorial on it here: vimeo.com/14315821.

Okay, you have your content and your poster software open to a blank canvas. Here is how to envision the rule of thirds.

FIGURE 5.6 Black lines divided the page into thirds in both directions, while blue stars show where to place critical pieces

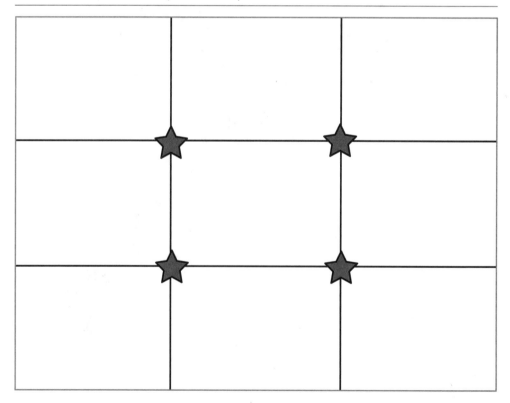

In this layout method, the blank canvas is mentally divided into a grid structure of thirds both horizontally and vertically, creating four points of intersection. These points are comfortable places to position images and important elements in the hierarchy of information. The rule of thirds tends to work better for light-text reporting, such as slideshows and report covers, because the image consumes so much of the area. It also works well in research poster contexts, where selected large text emphasizes the main message at those points of intersection.

FIGURE 5.7 The photograph of the principal is placed at an intersection of the dark lines, according to the Rule of Thirds

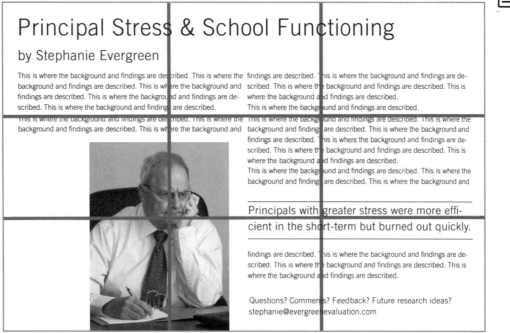

In the poster example shown above, the thick dark lines divide the page into vertical and horizontal thirds. Note that the image of the burned-out principal is located at one intersection of lines. At another intersection, I placed the key takeaway point from the study.

In more text-heavy circumstances, the rule of thirds can help determine ideal locations for data displays, tables, or other figures.

Figure 5.8 arranges the graph at the lower left intersection. You probably noticed that the location of this data display is roughly the same as the Gutenberg Diagram recommendations. No coincidence there.

Emphasis Techniques

Generally, it is effective to work with a grid structure consistently arranged according to one of these models where the most important information is prominent. Remember way back in

FIGURE 5.8 The graph is roughly located at the intersecting lines

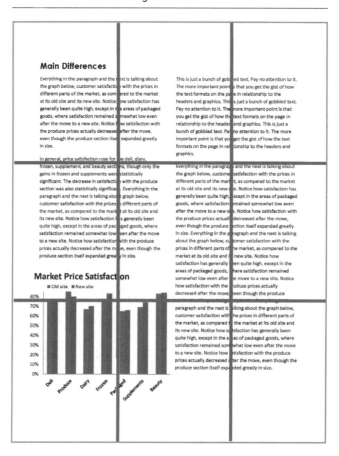

Chapter 1 when we discussed the power of graphic design to draw early attention? This is precisely where that power comes in handy. The addition of graphic elements like size, color, and orientation also creates key positions by cueing attention (Wolfe & Horowitz, 2004). Manipulation of those elements is another successful strategy for emphasizing information in the hierarchy and supporting comprehension of the text. Secondary, supportive, and explanatory information is dialed back with decreases in size, contrast, and/or position on the page.

The poster example shown in Figure 5.7 contains the type of preferred hierarchy. The title is the largest thing on the poster. Key information is smaller than the title but larger than the narrative text. Then the explanatory narrative is much smaller. Type size was used to establish the hierarchy, just as in the graphs in Chapter 3.

In other applications of these ideas, the title typically gets the most emphasis, because it is often the highest in the page's hierarchy of information. The author's name and institutional affiliation are deemphasized because they are less important (sorry). Then, to keep the reading flow moving, the start of the main narrative section might be given secondary emphasis through techniques like outdenting, drop cap (enlarged first letter), or color blocking.

Arrows, guiding lines, numbering systems, movement in a photo, and other directive graphic elements also help guide the selective attention of the reader toward the author's intended areas of emphasis (Treisman, 1988). Such emphasis and guided direction improve attention and focus, lead to faster processing, and increase comprehension by providing visual cues to the reader. These steps activate more visual processing schemas, promoting retention and recall from long-term memory (Woodman, Vecera, & Luck, 2003).

Do I Need to Do Anything About Margins?

You have probably noticed that most of the examples in this book leave open swaths of empty space on one side of a page. Thus, you might be thinking what a waste of paper. Those of us who are efficient minded tend to want to cram in as much information as possible onto as few pages as possible, and maybe in doing so we would actually decrease the number of pages in the report, save a couple of trees, and fall within our semester printing limit at the campus computing lab. This might be true—but it does not assist reader cognition.

> **Guiding Idea**
>
> Lines of narrative text are 8 to 12 words in length

When thinking about grids and line length and functionality, we need to keep in mind how the design hinders or enhances readability for the audience.

Line Length

Comprehension studies (Wheildon, 2005) show that readers can best track a narrative when lines are 8 to 12 words in length (the range is because it depends on the choice in typeface, type size, and number of columns). For those of us who like long words, let me translate: for optimal reading conditions, it is about 50 to 80 characters per line. Longer lines make it difficult for readers to track even when there is a strong axis of orientation, which means that they falter a bit when trying to finish one line of narrative text and start another. Shorter lines tend to create too many hyphenated words, distracting the reader and breaking up the reading flow. So, that is the reason why a large margin on one side of the page, despite potential ecological impacts, literally makes more sense.

These suggestions align with APA (2010) guidelines, which specify that the line length should be a maximum of 6.5 inches (the default setting of one column with 1 inch margins on all sides, using default font settings), thus restricting line lengths shorter than that maximum is acceptable. The MLA style guide (2009) proposes 1-inch margins all around, so keep that restriction in mind when aiming for publication in an MLA journal. Of course, follow whatever directions you are given for your dissertation or journal article (probably 1-inch margins), but consider more reader-friendly margins when publishing elsewhere.

FIGURE 5.9 A wide margin reduces line length to a comfortable size

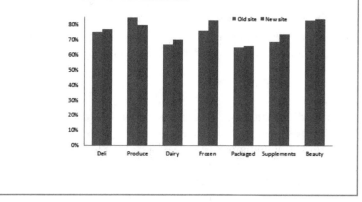

In the example above, the left margin is set at 2 inches, with regular 1-inch margins on the rest of the page. Using multiple columns also works, depending on the size of the text. To meet this guiding idea using columns, I had to adjust the default settings in Word. For a two-column setting, I had to decrease the font size to 10 points, decrease the margins from 1 inch to 0.75 inches on the left and right, and I had to increase the width of each column to 3.4 inches.

On wider layouts, such as for a research poster, effective data presentation has a couple of variations. In one method, the poster's grid structure makes use of columns. In the example below, the grid structure includes three columns, with the image taking up one of those three. The main narrative text spanning across the other two columns is set in 48-point font size, which is pretty large. Subtitle and callout text is set in 72 points.

FIGURE 5.10 A wide margin on a poster creates adequate line length and leaves space for a picture

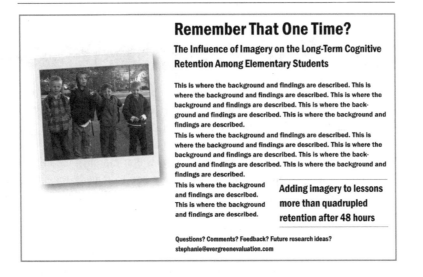

In more traditional poster arrangements, where pictures are not so large or not present at all, the narrative text fills the poster, from left side to right side. To meet this guiding idea, the font is very large in size, think 72 points, making it easy to read at a distance. But such a large size can make it difficult for people to stand physically close to the poster and engage the researcher in conversation. In that case, a grid structure is still used for organization, but the text itself is broken into a multiple column format for optimal reading.

FIGURE 5.11 Appropriate line length on a poster can also be achieved through the use of columns

In Figure 5.11, the narrative text is set in 38 point. Smaller fonts might be more comfortable (or even mandated by the conference organization)—just use more columns to arrange the text so that line length stays appropriate.

Rule of the Dollar Bill

Some graphic designers refer to the "Rule of the Dollar Bill." This rule says that if a block of text is larger than the size of a dollar bill, it is too big. At that size, it appears intimidating to the reader, presuming it takes a lot of cognitive work to read and digest the information (unless the reader has a lot of invested interest, such as when your professor grades your papers). Graphic designers suggest the report author widen margins, create more paragraphs, add some graphic elements, and simplify language to remedy the situation. The Rule of the Dollar Bill might not be backed up by research, but it is a good barometer to determine if text should be broken up when working with 8.5- × 11-inch documents. Convey the same intention of supporting the reader when working with larger documents, such as research posters.

How Should I Justify Text?

We discussed how important it is for readers to have a consistent axis of orientation when reading long narrative passages. In Latin alphabet cultures, this means the lines of the body text should all begin in alignment along the left, what is referred to as left justified.

Guiding Idea

Narrative text is left or full justified

FIGURE 5.12   This text is aligned to the left, or left justified

Lorem ipsum dolor sit amet, consectetur adipiscing elit. Nullam et purus vel elit luctus condimentum. Ut egestas justo arcu, eget lacinia mauris. Suspendisse potenti. Etiam commodo fringilla ultricies. Fusce non nunc id dolor semper lobortis ut at felis. Sed est erat, porttitor sed convallis eget, pellentesque ut orci. Nam euismod eros a tortor consequat sit amet accumsan sem vestibulum. Vestibulum ante ipsum primis in faucibus orci luctus et ultrices posuere cubilia Curae; Quisque tempor accumsan tristique. Mauris a magna vel nisl facilisis blandit. Morbi id neque sed metus rutrum rutrum vitae ut ante. Aliquam erat volutpat. Nam sollicitudin ornare dolor ut consectetur. In hac habitasse platea dictumst. Mauris euismod sapien non eros dapibus hendrerit.

The type of placement shown in Figure 5.12 is left justified with a ragged right edge. See how the right edge of the block of text undulates in and out? That is the ragged edge, which is the easiest format to read for normal readers. For narrative body text, you want to make certain that the text has a strong axis of orientation on the left side. To some people, the ragged right edge communicates a bit of informality when used in written reporting, despite its strong legibility (Lupton, 2004).

When I work with clients or colleagues who are in academia, I find that generally their preference is for a more formal look. More formality is reflected by a two-column, fully justified placement, which is often found in journals. Full justification is the setting where the lines both begin and end in alignment and the software adjusts the spacing between words within each line. For highly fluent readers, this setting is shown to best support comprehension (Wheildon, 2005).

However, as you can see, there are some graphic design issues at play when we use both full justification and columns. I drew in some blue lines to highlight what many of you probably already find somewhat irritating. Graphic designers call these gaps in typesetting or midsentence spacing issues "white rivers." I am certain you can find a few more of these in this block of text. They were given a name precisely because they are so distracting to the reader. Most certainly, you want the reader paying attention to your words, not the spaces between your words!

If you are really adamant about using full justification, you have some options to remedy the white rivers. You can either widen the columns, move to a single column, or decrease the size of the text by a half point. Any of these options make room for more words per line and then the software better adjusts to the spaces between words.

Here is the same text fully justified in one column. Most of the white rivers have gone away. However, the white rivers are especially common when the author is prone (ahem) to using long words. So, it is something you need to review throughout your document when you finish writing, if you are committed to full justification. Even so, APA (2010) guidelines prefer that text be left justified with a ragged right edge rather than fully justified.

FIGURE 5.13 This text is aligned on both the left and right, which sometimes leads to ugly spacing

Lorem ipsum dolor sit amet, consectetur adipiscing elit. Nullam et purus vel elit luctus condimentum. Ut egestas justo arcu, eget lacinia mauris. Suspendisse potenti. Etiam commodo fringilla ultricies. Fusce non nunc id dolor semper lobortis ut at felis. Sed est erat, porttitor sed convallis eget, pellentesque ut orci. Nam euismod eros a tortor consequat sit amet accumsan sem vestibulum. Vestibulum ante ipsum primis in faucibus orci luctus et ultrices posuere cubilia Curae; Quisque tempor accumsan tristique. Mauris a magna vel nisl facilisis blandit. Morbi id neque sed metus rutrum rutrum vitae ut ante. Aliquam erat volutpat. Nam sollicitudin ornare dolor ut consectetur. In hac habitasse platea dictumst. Mauris euismod sapien non eros dapibus hendrerit.

FIGURE 5.14 Full justification looks better on wider columns

Lorem ipsum dolor sit amet, consectetur adipiscing elit. Nullam et purus vel elit luctus condimentum. Ut egestas justo arcu, eget lacinia mauris. Suspendisse potenti. Etiam commodo fringilla ultricies. Fusce non nunc id dolor semper lobortis ut at felis. Sed est erat, porttitor sed convallis eget, pellentesque ut orci. Nam euismod eros a tortor consequat sit amet accumsan sem vestibulum. Vestibulum ante ipsum primis in faucibus orci luctus et ultrices posuere cubilia Curae; Quisque tempor accumsan tristique. Mauris a magna vel nisl facilisis blandit. Morbi id neque sed metus rutrum rutrum vitae ut ante. Aliquam erat volutpat. Nam sollicitudin ornare dolor ut consectetur. In hac habitasse platea dictumst. Mauris euismod sapien non eros dapibus hendrerit.

Proper use of centered alignment is theoretically sparse but is actually used quite often. Centered alignment should be reserved for rare and formal occasions, such as funeral ceremony agendas, wedding announcements, and graduation party invitations. Centered alignment is the default setting for titles in slideshows and graphs, but there is little evidence that such alignment is useful. None of the layout models we discussed in this book identify the top center of the page as a natural location for important information.

In slideshows, you can change the default layout to a different alignment by working with the Slide Master.

In PowerPoint 2010 on a PC, click on the *View* tab and then select *Slide Master* from the options shown in the *Master Views* group. Here you find a cascading string of possible slide layout options.

FIGURE 5.15 Adjust the justification settings in the master view to make subsequent formatting much easier

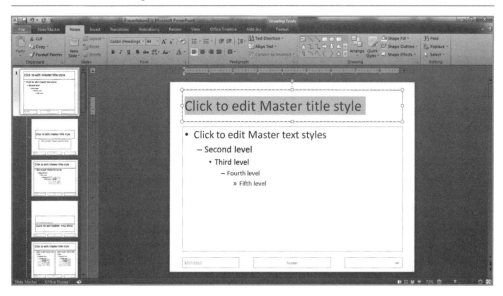

Working in the first slide shown—the largest one with the numeral 1 by it—will apply the changes to the rest of the slides in the string. So here, highlight the title text, navigate back to the Home tab, and click on the left justify button. (While you are here, resize and reposition the content text boxes so less fits or delete them altogether. At the very least, delete the bullets!) In just a few pages, we apply these techniques to graphs.

How Can I Align Using Typical Software?

Alignment is an attention-grabbing feature quickly picked up by a reader, so be sure elements start in the same place on each page unless you choose to misalign something on purpose.

Guiding Idea

Alignment is consistent

Achieving Consistent Placement

In Figure 5.1, the Greenpeace grid example, I inserted lines over the figures to demonstrate how to conceptually divide a page into a grid. In some software programs (especially the expensive graphic design ones) it is possible to draw those lines right in the program and then snap elements to the grid.

PowerPoint also has guidelines that can be activated. Look under the *View* tab in the *Show* group and check the box next to *Guides*. The lines can be moved to your specification

around the slide, but there is only one vertical and one horizontal line, which can be insufficient when there are several pieces to arrange, such as a text box, an icon, and an image.

Microsoft Word does not have guidelines at all, so it can be a bit tricky to achieve consistent alignment. Here are two strategies to master consistency using the mainstream software you own.

Use the Size and Position Function

FIGURE 5.16   Graphics are in different sizes and places on each page, leading to an inconsistent and unpolished layout

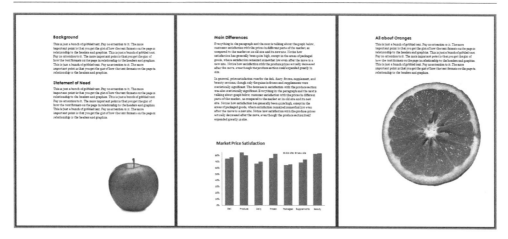

This is a mock report I developed to talk about arranging photos. A typical report does not necessarily have images on each page, but I included them here for demonstration purposes. You can see in this example that the first two graphics appear to be in roughly the same position. But I just pasted in the image of the orange—how can I get it consistently arranged?

The first step is to arrange one page in exactly the format and look that you want. In my word-processing program, I zoomed out to view the first few pages simultaneously. Then I clicked on the first image—the apple—and moved it around so that it looked to my eye to be in a position that worked with my grid structure.

It may also help to briefly turn on the gridlines, which overlay on the document and help with precise placement. In Word 2010 on a PC, click in the *View* tab and then check the box by gridlines in the *Show* group. Gridlines are annoying, though, so turn this feature off when you don't need it.

Now that the first picture is in place, I can right-click on that picture and choose *Size* and *Position*. A box opens that looks like Figure 5.17.

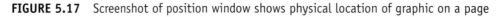

FIGURE 5.17   Screenshot of position window shows physical location of graphic on a page

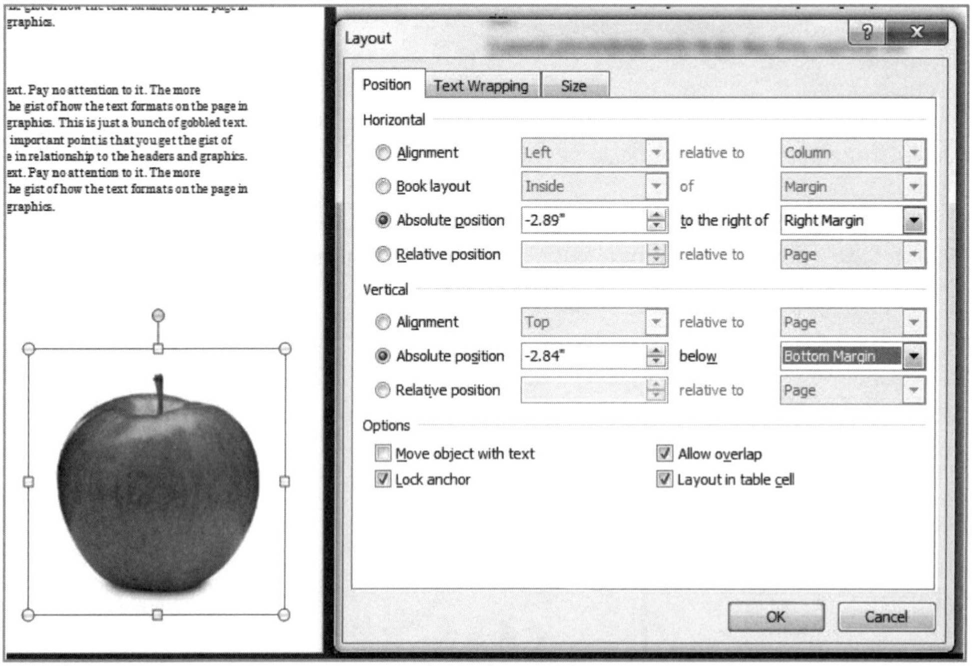

In the *Position* tab, Word shows me the exact page dimensions that identify where this graphic is located. Do you see how there is also a dropdown menu, allowing me to relate the image's location to various parts of the document? For right now, just write down those numbers and menu options. Sit tight—I come right back to this in a sentence or two.

Keeping the same box open, I can click on the Size tab to get the measurements for my image. The apple is 3.25" × 3.25." Jot that down, too.

Now, I close that box and right click on the image of the orange and choose *Size* and *Position*. Here is where I type in the same numbers, starting with size. (In real life, when I was making this example, I typed in 3.25" in the height box, but the orange was not a perfect square, so I used the cropping tool to trim either side.) After the size matches, I move over to the Position tab and enter the same dimensions as the apple. This forces the orange image to the same location on the page as the apple.

In this improvement, the arrangement is consistent. Even better, the same procedure works throughout the Office software programs. This process also works for graphs (investigate the *Wrap* options) or any other type of graphic. Because the graph in Figure 5.18 is a different shape than the fruit, I need to relate my position dimensions to the bottom and right parts of the page.

Using this method, I achieve alignment with words and text, and maintain a grid structure. The same consistency is critically important between slides for a seamless viewing

FIGURE 5.18   Adjusting the size and position of graphics achieves a clearer and more effective presentation

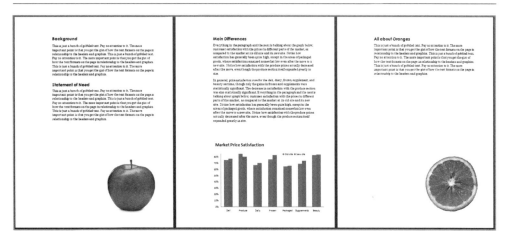

experience. This method is not as automatic as in specialized layout programs, but it allows you to sort of fake a grid system and ensure a consistent arrangement using the tools already at your disposal.

Should I Anchor the Image?

Note in Figure 5.17 one of the selections in the dropdown menu is the ability to choose whether to anchor the image to the text or to the page. This is a decision point where the research in cognitive processing does not play nicely with the common practices in graphic design. Cognitive researchers suggest you anchor the image to the text so that no matter how much, say, introductory text is added to the front of the report section, which pushes your content to new pages, the image always travels with its associated text. As we discussed in Chapter 2, it is preferable for reader comprehension if the graphic is very near its associated text. But graphic designers recommend that images appear in consistent places on the pages where they are present, caring less about proximity to associated text, and thus hope you anchor your picture to the page so that it is unmovable, even if introductory text is added. If images are less frequent in written reports, I am more inclined to let them move with their text.

Use Groups

In part, graphic design practice is based in the theory of Gestalt, which was adopted to predict how specific arrangements of information influence interpretation by the brain (Tourangeau, Couper, & Conrad, 2004, 2007). The five main

Guiding Idea

Grouped items logically belong together

Gestalt-based principles are middle means typical, left and top mean first, near means related, up means good, and like means close. For example, "like means close" indicates that items that appear close together are interpreted by the reader as belonging to one another, whether the likeness is in color, font, size, or physical proximity. This interpretation particularly supports the ability to comprehend graphs and other graphic elements; grouping or chunking data in graphs leads to a better ability to describe patterns in data (Woodman, Vecera, & Luck, 2003).

FIGURE 5.19   Chunks of data are marked by use of a dot and line above the chunk and as much space as possible between chunks

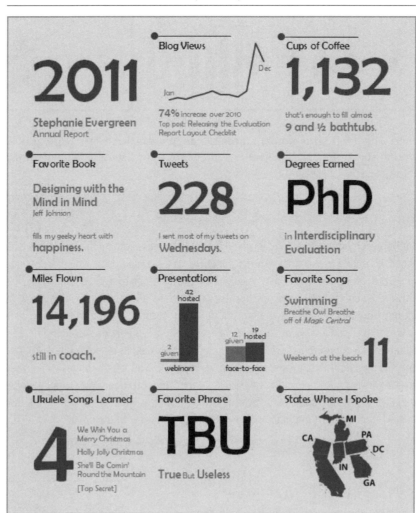

In my personal annual report dashboard from 2011, there are clearly 12 chunks or groups of information. A couple of features help to make those groups obvious. First, the dot-and-line

combination placed over the top of 11 of the 12 chunks demarcates a new group of information. The first chunk has no dot-and-line combination to visually identify it as the heading—remember left and top signify first. The physical proximity of each dot-and-line combination to its associated text and graphics also contributes to a sense of a cluster or chunk. Near means related. Internally, the elements in each chunk are physically closer together than the space between each chunk. This grouping strategy is sometimes referred to by graphic designers as "squish and separate" (Samara, 2007). We want the elements in the chunk squished closer together and then separated from surrounding chunks. In this way, empty space helps organize the information into more digestible pieces. Finally, decoding is aided by the grid structure. The dashboard clearly has four rows and three columns. Within each row, the dot-and-line combinations are aligned. Within each column, the words in each grouping begin in the same location. Grouping pieces is effective outside of infographics and dashboards, as well.

Grouping Graphics with Text Grouped items are interpreted as one chunk of information. When combining graphics and text, position the pieces so that logical items are placed together. This sounds pretty abstract at this point, I know. At a somewhat macro level, effective grouping is when we ensure the data's narrative and display arrange well on a single page. This arrangement is encouraged by the MLA style guide (2009), which suggests figures be placed as close as possible to their related text. To make that explanation more concrete, look at several combinations of graphics with text.

Here are three possible ways to lay out the same elements.

FIGURES 5.20, 5.21, and 2.22 Three different configurations of report pieces on a single page—which best fits the Gutenberg Diagram?

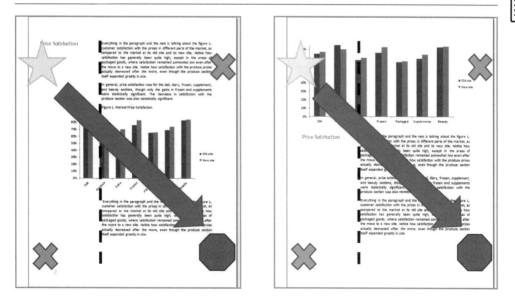

(Continued)

FIGURES 5.20, 5.21, and 2.22 (Continued)

All of these arrangements pretty much fit the reading gravity we desire, according to the Gutenberg Diagram. The first option is okay, but the placement of the graph breaks the axis of orientation. The second version in Figure 5.21 is another option, and the axis of orientation is kept intact. But, since a reader's eyes start in the upper left anyway, try capitalizing on the attraction of graphs and move it elsewhere. In the third version, the title starts us off on the page and reading gravity carries the reader through the narrative text. We have the graph in the typically ignored corner, but because graphs are so eye-catching, we actually activate that corner for the reader.

Another common combination of graphics and text for researchers is in the ubiquitous logic model. Here, we typically have column headings running across the top of the diagram, as a way to identify the main conceptual categories, from Inputs to Long-Term Outcomes (we can argue about the merits of logic models and their components some other time). Program elements are then detailed under each column. Thus, we have groups of information.

With the logic model, we can add graphic elements to more clearly signal groups. Spacing is one subtle but essential way to indicate that the columns are distinct groups. Note how considerable berth is maintained between each column. The second way I indicated distinct groupings was through the inclusion of a graphic element—the large background boxes under the Activities column. I wanted to visually represent that the program activities were divided into two phases. By inserting a large rectangle to encompass the

FIGURE 5.23   Logic model elements are grouped by space and color

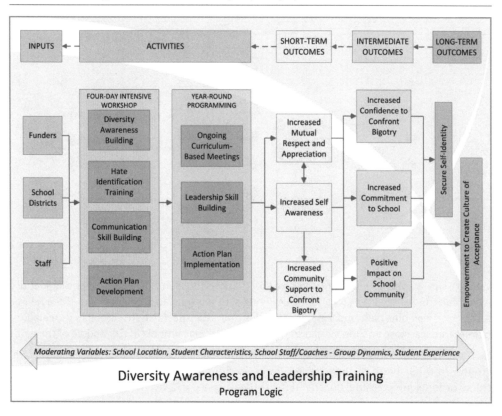

Source: © 2009 Reprinted with permission from DALT.

activity boxes and adding a short label, I more clearly grouped the elements that belong together. Using large graphic elements in the background is an effective method for grouping other visual elements, whether blocks of text or images. The third way I expressed grouping in this logic model is through color—each column has its own. As discussed in Chapter 4, you have to be careful when placing text on a color background, but to see what it looks like in this logic model, head to the website (www.sagepub.com/evergreen).

Grouping Graphics with Graphics Let's return to this "squish and separate" idea for a moment. Though it is less common, sometimes graphics are paired with graphics and their careful handling is important to user cognition. For example, look at these playing cards my son brought home one day. Notice the problem (aside from the fact that they are shaped like snowmen)?

Guiding Idea

Empty area is allocated on each page

FIGURE 5.24   The elements on these playing cards are poorly grouped and can lead to confusion

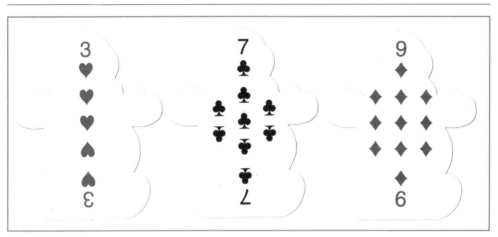

We have two graphic groups here: the category markers (the symbol and number that identify which suit this card belongs to) and the counting symbols (placed in the middle—three hearts, seven clubs, and nine diamonds, in this example). The issue, quickly noticed, is that the category markers are too close and too similar to the actual counting symbols in the middle of the card.

Now, with these playing cards, we are limited in our ability to distinguish these two graphic groups. In other parts of this chapter, more exciting possibilities like applying different colors or fonts are possible, but that defeats the purpose in a deck of cards.

When working with pairs of graphics, you want to create more empty space on the page, or slide, or card by squishing together the things that belong in one group and separating that group from the groups around it. The empty space serves as the organizing element. With these cards, the category markers could be much smaller. Or much larger. Or just positioned further away from the counting symbols in the middle. The counting symbols in the middle could also be squished closer together.

In this next example (see Figures 5.25, 5.26, and 5.27), there is a lot happening on a single slide. Typically, we want less content, but occasionally there are times when several pieces are needed. In that instance, when dealing with a greater number of elements, grouping and grids become all the more important. The program in this example is composed of five main strategies and discussing these strategies is a common topic for program staff when making presentations to outside parties. So, we present text with graphics with text with graphics.

The first slide on the left shows what a weak arrangement looks like. Nothing is aligned well. The slide looks sloppy, and this arrangement imparts the same message about the organization, which definitely does not suit the good work of Project LAUNCH.

The second slide to the right shows how the arrangement improves with the addition of a grid. I divided the slide into five columns and three rows and started arranging the different pieces so that each element fit into a cell on the grid. Note the Project LAUNCH logo actually fills two cells—that is fine, as long as it is exactly two. I also shifted the text boxes toward

FIGURES 5.25, 5.26, and 5.27

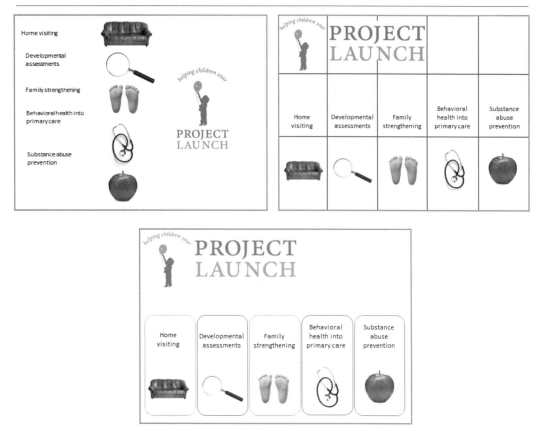

the bottom of their cells so that they were squished a bit closer to their associated pictures. If we remove the gridlines, we can see how the grid structure vastly improved the quality of the slide. Still, it is a lot of information; it is still possible to group the associated parts to more clearly communicate their message.

The bottom slide illustrates how grouping can work when there is not much space to separate the groups. We used empty rectangles to enclose the two items that are associated, more obviously creating five distinct aspects of the program. Even though there are a lot of elements happening on this slide, the organizational structure better communicates to the viewer that the author has a logical rationale for the talk.

Grouping Text with Text Similarly, when working with multiple groups of text, leave plenty of space between groups.

I took the picture in Figure 5.28 in a bathroom stall in Traverse City, Michigan. I literally closed the door, saw the sign, and thought, "Oh my god, what kind of ramshackle place is this that doesn't have a smoking alarm with sound?"

FIGURE 5.28   Poor grouping on this sign can lead to confusion (or maybe it's just me)

Of course, it may just be me, but the message is impaired because the first text group ("No Smoking") needs to be more distinct from the second text group ("Alarm Will Sound"). More space is needed between these two groups, as well as some other type of distinction (i.e., larger font size for the first text group). At the least, a greater difference between the groups makes it less alarming.

Here is the corresponding lesson for researchers: when we use headings to signal the organization of a report, make the heading really, really, really, clearly different from the narrative text. There are many options when working with headings, so remember that you can use generous space, and font, color, and other emphasis techniques to make them obviously distinguishable from the narrative.

In this example, the headings are emphasized by choosing a different font and making them bold (review the Type chapter). They are also emphasized by adding empty space. Space around a heading is created in two ways. There is the space before the heading, where it is preceded by other report content, and the space after the heading, where its corresponding text follows. Because the heading is more closely related to its own text, it should be physically closer to that text than to the preceding narrative that is less conceptually related. In Figure 5.29, the heading for Statement of Need is further away from the previous paragraph about Background.

FIGURE 5.29   Allow more spacing before a heading than after it, to group it with its associated narrative

Background

This is just a bunch of gobbled text. Pay no attention to it. The more important point is that you get the gist of how the text formats on the page in relationship to the headers and graphics. This is just a bunch of gobbled text. Pay no attention to it. The more important point is that you get the gist of how the text formats on the page in relationship to the headers and graphics. This is just a bunch of gobbled text. Pay no attention to it. The more important point is that you get the gist of how the text formats on the page in relationship to the headers and graphics.

Statement of Need

This is just a bunch of gobbled text. Pay no attention to it. The more important point is that you get the gist of how the text formats on the page in relationship to the headers and graphics. This is just a bunch of gobbled text. Pay no attention to it. The more important point is that you get the gist of how the text formats on the page in relationship to the headers and graphics. This is just a bunch of gobbled text. Pay no attention to it. The more important point is that you get the gist of how the text formats on the page in relationship to the headers and graphics.

Here is how I established those dimensions in Word 2010 on a PC:

FIGURE 5.30   This screenshot shows how to adjust the spacing before and after a heading

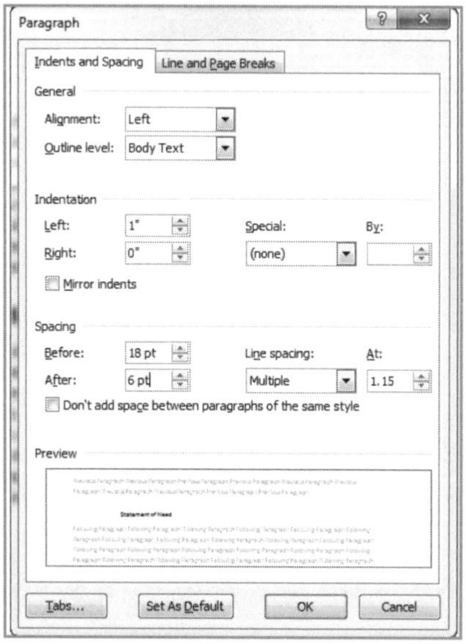

If we think of the heading and its text as a group, they should be more squished and so in the *Spacing After* box, I decreased the size to 6 point so that the space after the heading is smaller, bringing the heading closer to the text. That text group should be further away from other text groups, so the *Spacing Before* the heading is increased to 18 points. Adjusting the spacing between groups of narrative text leaves adequate empty space and serves to better communicate the report's organization.

When Is It Okay to Break the Rules?

In the context of arrangement, we can sometimes increase audience understanding by purposely ignoring rules about orientation, grids, and text justification. Look at another Ad Council advertisement that succeeds in defying the rules we just established with the somewhat rare use of right justification. The MLA style guide does not want you to see this.

FIGURE 5.31   Right justified text can be effective in some circumstances

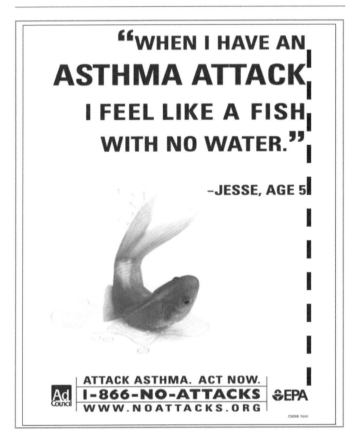

Source: © 2012 Reprinted with permission from the Environmental Protection Agency.

Notice here how the text at the top of the ad is aligned on the right side. The axis of orientation is drawn in with the dotted line. It is an unnatural way of reading for most people in Western cultures. In this ad, it still works well without impacting legibility too much because the phrasing is short. Additionally, the discomfort of the text placement, which makes us work against reading gravity, actually contributes to and reinforces the sense they are trying to convey in this advertisement about raising awareness for asthma. Beautifully done. The advertisement used right justification to break the rules and gets away with it because by doing so, they consciously contributed to the overall tone of the document. So right justification works sometimes, particularly if the wording is short and if the conveyed message is meant to relay a bit of discomfort. At times, graphic designers also use right justification to convey a hip, or youthful, or unique mood, but such uses tend to be initiated by a desire to appear interesting, and attract early attention, often at the expense of reader cognition. Therefore, it is best to keep it short and sweet, limited to bursts of text like callouts, or headings, or titles.

Nonetheless, rule breaking can be effective when it is done selectively for emphasis purposes.

FIGURE 5.32 A different orientation can both draw attention and group items

Research Report Layout Guidelines

This checklist is meant to be used as a diagnostic guide to identify elements of evaluation reports that could be enhanced using graphic design best practices and/or the assistance of a graphic design expert. Suggestions are best suited for those using standard Microsoft Word software.

Graphics

Pictures/graphic elements are present
Multimode learning increases chance at storage of info in long-term memory because it eases cognitive load of body text. Choose pictures or graphics related to your topic. Graphics include, but shouldn't be limited to, tables and charts.

Graphics are near associated text
If readers must flip around to interpret between text and graphic, comprehension will be impaired.

Graphics are simple
Less visual noise leads to better assimilation. Eliminate gradation, textures, or graphics as backgrounds. Segment complex graphics into smaller chunks.

Size corresponds to changes in meaning
Use, for example, larger pictures on chapter start pages. In graphing, for example, be sure height of columns proportionately represents data.

Graphics direct toward text
Use the power of an image to direct the reader's gaze from the image to the associated text. Eyes in a photo, for example, should look inward at text.

Tips

Pictures and graphics related to your content will make your content more memorable.

Choose pictures from quality sources, like paid websites. Watermarks or fuzzy images are signs of an amateur.

Use a cover page at the beginning of a report. This is a good place for a very large graphic.

Font

Text fonts are used for narrative text
Use serif fonts. Nothing with lots of graphic detail.

Long reading is in 9-11 point size
Studies have shown that 11 point text is easiest to read at length, but it can depend on the font.

Body text has stylistic uniformity
Each text section has unbolded, normal text in sentence case (no all caps), except in short areas of intentional emphasis. This supports undistracted reading.

Line spacing is 11-13 points
For lines within paragraph, generally choose 1-2 points larger than the size of the body text.

In Figure 5.32, those elements that typically are viewed as the headings are turned on their side and dragged into the margin (what do we call these—"sidings"?). The vertical line also assists in grouping the text that belongs under the "Graphics" section. In this instance, such a rebellious arrangement actually works to better support use of the guidelines in the hand-out, because a reader can see the main areas of guidance at a glance.

At times, outdenting, or consigning the start of a line way out to the left of the narrative text, is also an effective way to bend the rules. While we usually want all narrative text left-aligned, in this situation, purposeful misalignment brings the reader's eye to those textual points. Outdenting emphasizes.

FIGURE 5.33   Outdented first sentences help structure a page

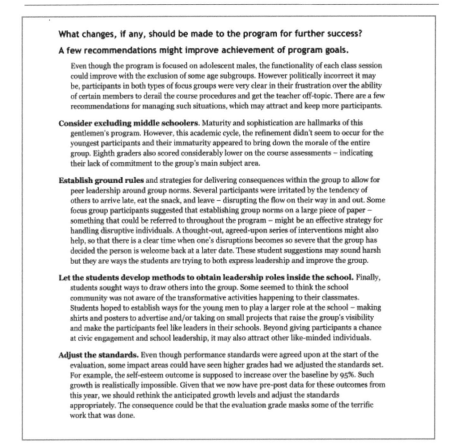

This particular example is depicting the part of the report where the author delivers the study's recommendations for improvement. For evaluators, recommendations are often the toughest aspect of the study to get adopted by a client. It probably does not help that we tend to bury the recommendations on page 104, but we will save that discussion for another book. Suffice it to say here that the recommendations are much harder to miss because they are now bolded and outdented. Now, if every paragraph begins this way, then you lose the effect. But, if we reserve outdenting (or any emphasis technique, for that matter) for only our most important points, even a reader who is flipping through the report pages is fixated on the recommendations because of their arresting misalignment.

How Do I Apply These Ideas to Graphs?

The APA Guide knows what's up: "An attractive graphical display makes a scientific article a more effective presentation device" (2010, p. 126). But, as we know and have stated, it is not just about being attractive. Graphs organized with meaning and narrative have faster decoding times for the reader than disorganized graphs or those without context (Shah, Mayer, & Hegarty, 1999). As applied to graphs, effective data presentation also supports interpretation and prediction tasks better than weak graphs or tables, which suggests they play a role in improved and informed decision making (Meyer, Shamo, & Gopher, 1999). So, let's apply this chapter's guiding ideas to the arrangement of pieces in a data display.

Legend Placement

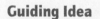

In Chapter 2, we discussed how graphics and text need to be placed right next to each other because when we flip back and forth between pages, it impairs the ability of our working memory to make sense of the associated words and images. Truly, the ideal situation for our brains is extremely close placement, which also applies to the words and images inside data displays. Whenever we have to seek-and-find to match up content, cognition is impaired. One way to get closer placement of words and images is to delete the legend. Yep, I just click on it and hit "delete."

Guiding Idea

Grouped items logically belong together

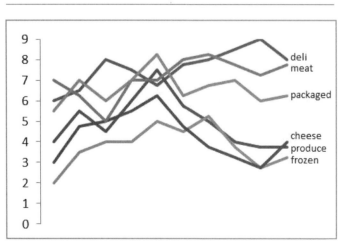

FIGURE 5.34   In lieu of a legend, the lines are directly labeled

In Figure 5.34, I inserted text boxes directly over the graph with the identifying word from the legend, so it is totally obvious which line associates with which text box, thus eliminating the need for the legend. Cognition remains supported.

A related concept works with stacked bar or column charts. You can reduce confusion by placing the legend across the top of the chart (in the case of bars) so that the colors in the legend are laid out in the same order as the colors in the stacked bars.

In Excel, you can even reposition and line up the legend so that it matches the length of the bars by clicking on the legend to activate and resize it.

FIGURE 5.35 Reposition legends so they align with the order of the bars

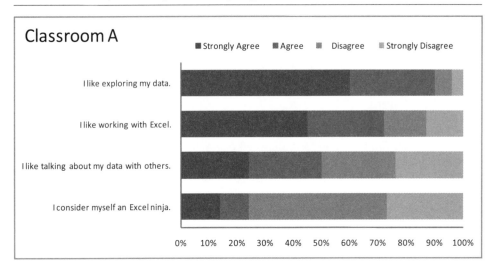

FIGURE 5.36 Directly label the bars on their first appearance

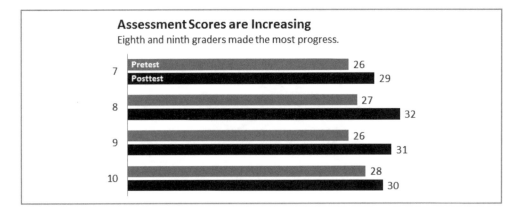

Simpler graphs, such as bar or column varieties, leave room for additional customization, resulting in a clearer presentation.

In typical default chart production, the labels for the two bars shown here, "Pretest" and "Posttest," are hanging off to the right, next to tiny squares filled with their associated colors. You can delete that legend and insert text boxes right over the bars that include the proper legend label. In this example, it really only has to be done once, for 7th graders here, to establish the logic of the graph. A reader can immediately interpret the remaining bars without additional labeling or having to go back and forth between the bars and the legend.

Label Placement

If you use Excel to generate a graph, it does this horrible thing. You have seen it. You probably sat down, highlighted some survey data, and asked Excel to generate a bar graph for you. When the data labels are lengthy, for example when dealing with question prompts from a survey, the graph ends up looking like Figure 5.37.

FIGURE 5.37 Excel uses centered justification on labels that spill over to a second line

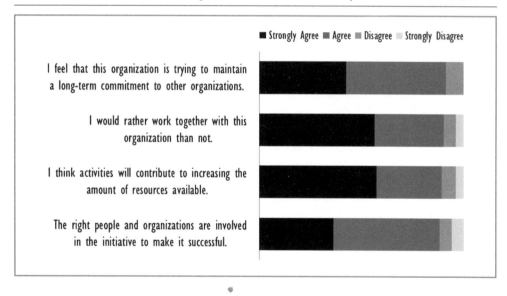

Excel automatically center justifies the data labels. While Excel excels at customization in many areas, it does not provide a way to uncenter those labels. As we note throughout this chapter, center alignment is hard to read and can actually get in the way of reader cognition. One option is to remove some uncritical words from each data label, while attempting to preserve its meaning. That works in some cases, but there are certainly times when the entire label must be present, because it represents the question prompt, for example. APA guidelines also ask that the labels are written as closely as possible to the components they identify. Do not dismay—we can keep in step with the style manual and still improve presentation. Again, the solution in this case is to take control of the full array of Microsoft Office tools.

Delete those centered labels and insert your own with text boxes.

FIGURE 5.38 Retyping labels into text boxes allows you to manipulate the text justification

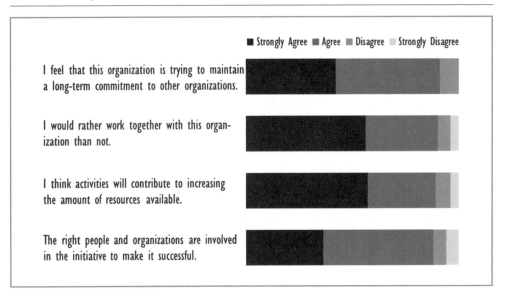

You can select all of the text box labels and align them so that they are equidistant from the bars. Simply estimate the pairing of each label with its bar, shooting to have the label and the bar horizontally centered with each other. When working with long data labels, we do not have to be at the mercy of Excel's default options. Be in control of your tools and use them to make data displays more meaningful.

Title Placement

We continue along this theme of owning your software by looking at how titles are placed. This example comes from my son's report card—not the one handed out by the school, (that's sensible), but the one generated by the standardized testing company. It was unintelligible and sent home without any explanatory narrative text. So, like any effective data presenter would, I opened my laptop and recreated it, guessing at what it was trying to tell me about my son, using the principles we've discussed throughout this book.

Guiding Idea

Narrative text is left or full justified

In the redesign, you can recognize that I eliminated the bottom axis and made my own data point labels to better reflect results that concern parents. I also used grayscale on the data labels that were of secondary importance in my hierarchy of information to downplay them a bit. They are still necessary reference points, but they aren't the most germane data at this

FIGURE 5.39 The original graph leaves a lot for a reader to muddle through.

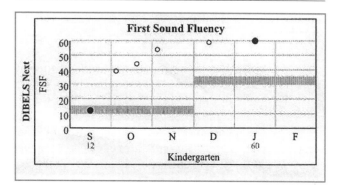

FIGURE 5.40 This redesigned graph uses a subtitle to explain the concepts being measured

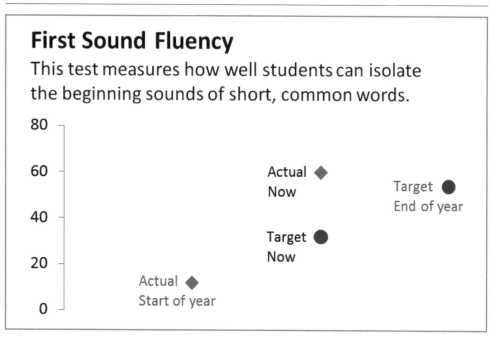

particular report card period. The new feature here is the effective change to the chart title. Rather than the default center alignment, I left justified the title. It is more inviting to read and it is in the top left corner (this location sounds familiar). I also added a short descriptive sentence, after I Googled what "first sound fluency" meant. First sound fluency is organizational jargon that is probably common knowledge to the folks working in the testing firm, but it is not equally obvious for most parents. To differentiate the heading from the descriptive sentence, I increased its size. Now, this chart can probably stand alone to be read unassisted by most parents.

Bar Arrangement

Guiding Idea

Important elements are prominent

To create a bar graph, we highlight the data in the spreadsheet table and ask the program to generate a graph. The graph arranges the bars in the order the data appear in the table. The problem is that we usually ordered the data in the table according to the order of the questions asked on the survey. This ordering may make perfect sense to those of us deeply embedded in the project but not to those outside of the project. We can do better to help the reader interpret the data display.

FIGURE 5.41 The order of the bars is not meaningful to a viewer

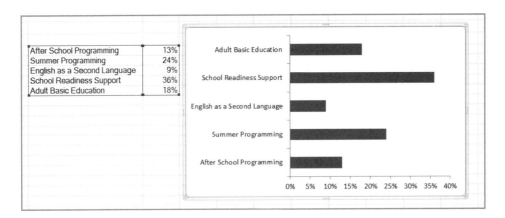

Instead, as the APA Guide suggests, place the bars in order from greatest to least. Sometimes there may be circumstances where you should defer to a different order like when the categories have a well-established scheme that is confusing if disrupted, such as listing states in alphabetical order.

Well, you cannot exactly move the bars around within the data display, but you can get them in the right order by sorting the data in the table.

FIGURE 5.42   This screenshot shows how to sort the spreadsheet data to produce a meaningfully ordered graph

First, highlight the rows containing data, not including the headings. Click the arrow by the *Sort and Filter* button in the *Editing* group on the *Home* tab to see *Custom Sort*. Choose the column with your values in it and select Smallest to Largest (in Excel, order the table backward to have it show up the right way in the graph). The graph automatically updates to reflect your new categorical order.

This same concept also works for better interpretation of stacked charts. In this case, I summed the positive responses (that is, Agree and Strongly Agree) and customized the sort order on the summed values.

FIGURE 5.43   In this case, the bars are ordered by the total responses in agreement, adding Strongly Agree and Agree together

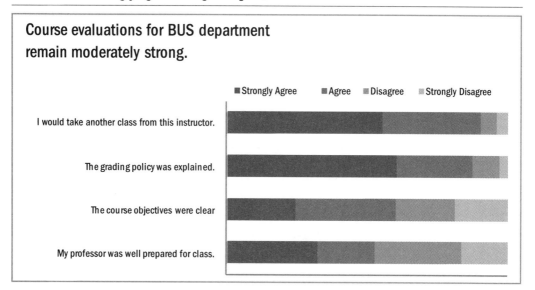

The summed values are not part of the display here—that is just a hidden part of my raw data table. But I can use it as a tool to help my stacked bar chart make more sense for the viewer. Also, notice that I manually moved the legend and placed it along the top of the bar chart so that the legend entries line up in the same sequence of the bars.

What Is the Bottom Line?

Ultimately, this chapter condenses to one key point: consistent arrangement of presentation elements makes our work more accessible and understandable for our audiences. When we intentionally place our elements in a logical fashion, we communicate our mental structure to our readers, increasing their ability to intake, digest, and retain the information we produce. Of course, all of this means that it is imperative to bring mental structure and logic to the organization of our reporting. Before turning on the computer to type a report, the report author should have the journey in mind. The main point, secondary points, and supporting evidence should be already identified in their order of importance. But you know what? You know that. Your key points are quite clear to you. You have been up to your eyeballs in this data for a long time. You know it inside and out. This chapter provides the guiding ideas you can put into place to make your well-structured mental architecture equally apparent to your audiences as well. Proper arrangement lets the reader peek inside your brain. What will they see? An effective data presenter.

KEY POINTS TO REMEMBER

Effective arrangement goes unnoticed. It is not a job for the glory-seekers. But weak arrangement looks sloppy and causes more confusion for an audience.

- Line length can hinder or support reading. Neither too long nor too short, aim for 8 to 12 words per line.

- Graphics draw attention first, wherever they are placed. Thus, position them to support their related narrative.

- A grid structure can help mentally dictate the lines to use to align report elements. Divide the page into rows and columns for straightforward document creation.

- Effective arrangement is also established through a hierarchy of information. Make the most important elements the largest and in key positions. Secondary information (callout points or headings, perhaps) is relatively smaller, but offset this material to be noticed. More supportive explanatory narrative is small, though captions and footnotes, the lowest in the hierarchy, can be even smaller.

- You are the captain of your software programs. Exploit the software to its full extent by inserting text boxes, or deleting axes, or whatever you need to do so that your data display keeps its statistically accurate representation but communicates with greater clarity.

HOW CAN I EXTEND THIS?

Check Out

Stephen Few's Graphic Design IQ Test (http://www.perceptualedge.com/files/GraphDesignIQ.html). This fun little quiz was created by the data visualization guru, Stephen Few. Just 10 questions long, it provides good (and bad) examples of data displays and reinforces many of the ideas presented throughout this book. Go give it a whirl.

Cole Nussbaumer, employee of Google, runs a great data visualization blog (http://www.storytellingwithdata.com/). She is a fan of using text boxes to make Excel do what you want and she refers to this technique as "brute force." Check out her blog posts for plenty of Excel-based inspiration.

ChartLabeler (http://www.appspro.com/Utilities/ChartLabeler.htm)_is a free Excel add-in made by AppsPro. My friend Agata introduced me to this tool, which makes existing data labels more flexible and easier to resize like a text box but also stays directly linked to table data and headings. Plug it in to your spreadsheets to make label arrangement a snap.

While the Gutenberg Diagram and the Rule of Thirds are popular layout options, there are others, such as the Z-layout and L-layout. Stephen Bradley blogged (http://www.vanseodesign.com/web-design/3-design-layouts/) about three layout options, including Gutenberg, and compared their strengths and weaknesses.

Try This

Fold a piece of paper into thirds. Unfold it, and fold it the other way in thirds. Unfold it. You now have nine squares with four intersecting points along the folds. Where the lines intersect is approximately where to place your main graphic. Go ahead and sketch it at one of those intersecting points and then write in a few keywords.

The same idea of creating a hierarchy of important information is also behind a great deal of web design. Check out your university's website and analyze its hierarchy. Notice what is located in the top left corner. It should be something of high importance (probably the university logo). Notice what text is the largest, and what does that signal about the way the web designers want you to navigate the site? It is almost certain that emphasis techniques were used on words that are relevant to prospective students and alumni.

Locate a few pieces of tracing paper (your university bookstore probably carries some in with the art supplies, but if not check a local art or hobby store). Use this tracing paper to regroup the graphic pieces on each slide from your last slideshow. Print out the slides, one per page. Then lay the tracing paper on top of the first slide and move it around to retrace and thus rearrange your pieces. Are your name and organizational affiliation spread apart?

Start by tracing your name where it should go and then move the tracing paper so that your name is repositioned over your organizational affiliation and retrace that. In the end, you should have a redesigned sketch of your slides, properly grouped, to take back to your computer for duplication in your slideshow software.

WHERE CAN I GO FOR MORE INFORMATION?

American Psychological Association. (2010). *Publication manual of the American Psychological Association* (6th ed.). Washington, DC: Author.

Lupton, E. (2004). *Thinking with type: A critical guide for designers, writers, editors, and students.* New York: Princeton Architectural Press.

Meyer, J., Shamo, M. K., & Gopher, D. (1999). Information structure and the relative efficacy of tables and graphs. *Human Factors, 41*(4), 570–588.

Modern Language Association of America. (2009). *MLA handbook for writers of research papers* (7th ed.). New York: Author.

Mueller-Brockmann, J. (1981). Grid and design philosophy. In *Grid systems in graphic design: A visual communication manual for graphic designers, typographers, and three-dimensional designers.* Niederteufen, Switzerland: Arthur Niggli. (Reprinted from *Graphic design theory,* by H. Armstrong, Ed., 2009. New York: Princeton Architectural Press)

Samara, T. (2007). *Design elements: A graphic style manual.* Beverly, MA: Rockport Press.

Shah, P., Mayer, R. E., & Hegarty, M. (1999). Graphs as aids to knowledge construction: Signaling techniques for guiding the process of graph comprehension. *Journal of Educational Psychology, 91*(4), 690–702.

Tourangeau, R., Couper, M. P., & Conrad, F. (2004). Spacing, position, and order: Interpretive heuristics for visual features of survey questions. *Public Opinion Quarterly, 68*(3), 368–393.

Tourangeau, R., Couper, M. P., & Conrad, F. (2007). Color, labels, and interpretive heuristics for response scales. *Public Opinion Quarterly, 71*(1), 91–112.

Treisman, A. (1988). Features and objects: The fourteenth Bartlett memorial lecture. *The Quarterly Journal of Experimental Psychology, 40a*(2), 201–237.

Wheildon, C. (2005). *Type and layout: Are you communicating or just making pretty shapes?* Mentone, Australia: The Worsley Press.

Wolfe, J. M., & Horowitz, T. S. (2004). What attributes guide the deployment of visual attention and how do they do it? *Nature, 5,* 1–7.

Woodman, G. F., Vecera, S. P., & Luck, S. J. (2003). Perceptual organization influences visual working memory. *Psychonomic Bulletin & Review, 10*(1), 80–87.

⑤SAGE researchmethods

The essential online tool for researchers from the world's leading methods publisher

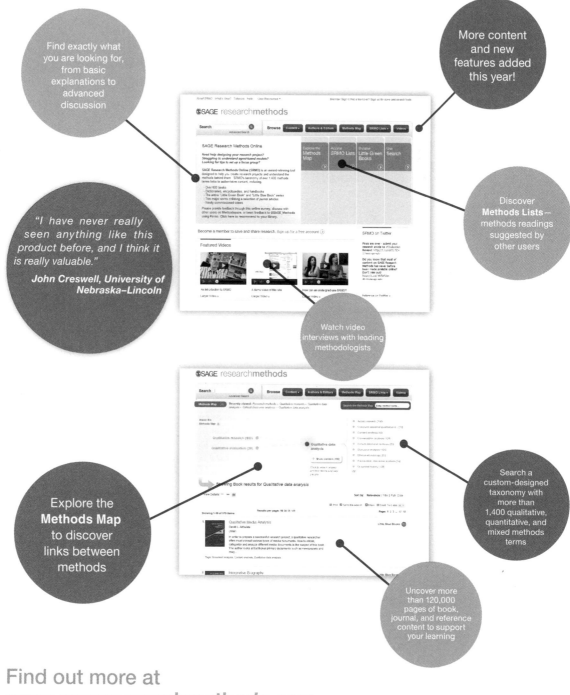

Find exactly what you are looking for, from basic explanations to advanced discussion

More content and new features added this year!

"I have never really seen anything like this product before, and I think it is really valuable."

John Creswell, University of Nebraska–Lincoln

Discover **Methods Lists**— methods readings suggested by other users

Watch video interviews with leading methodologists

Explore the **Methods Map** to discover links between methods

Search a custom-designed taxonomy with more than 1,400 qualitative, quantitative, and mixed methods terms

Uncover more than 120,000 pages of book, journal, and reference content to support your learning

Find out more at
www.sageresearchmethods.com

A Short Last Word on Presenting Data Effectively

Learning Objectives

After reading this chapter you will be able to:

- Pull together your design choices to make dissemination easier
- Feel confident about stepping away from traditional reporting formats
- Articulate the justification for spending your time on design
- Summarize the key points of this book

Now that you are nearly at the end of this book, you have learned a lot about how to present data effectively. You have probably reflected on some of your own reports and slideshows and criticized a few graphs from the newspaper. You may even be thinking ahead to your next research poster with excitement and anticipation. Good. You are going to rock it.

But, before you and I part ways, let's remember why we came here in the first place. If we recall the fundamental reasons for rethinking our data presentations, you are in a better position to justify your efforts to the skeptics that I hope you never meet. In this chapter, we identify the two main criticisms of effective data presentation and the three benefits you can name to address them.

Criticism: Trying to Look Slick

Benefit 1: Fits with How the Brain Operates

One of the criticisms that will be heard when you begin to redesign your data presentations is probably something along the lines of "nah, don't worry about that—we aren't trying to

look like a marketing agency here." I know. I have heard it. In fact, the single hard critique launched from the audience at my dissertation was that it appeared that most of the recommendations I made for good report layout were my personal opinions and aesthetic preferences. Through both research and examples, we demonstrated that good design choices are based in a user-centered perspective. Deeper than aesthetics, effective data presentation is about reworking our data so that it can be understood.

Weak data presentation is expensive. It is confusing. It misleads the audience. It turns off potential clients. It discourages interaction with your data.

Effective data presentation, by contrast, is clear and useful. It supports the audience's efforts at reading and cognition. It improves and bolsters decision making. It gets remembered.

Effective data presentation uses color to catch early attention, and it makes engagement easier by choosing fonts that are easy on the eye (or eye-brain). Effective data presentation arranges reporting elements in order to reduce the cognitive load on a reader and creates chunks of information that can be readily digested by working memory. Effective data presentation includes pictures, diagrams, and graphs to play off a reader's visual strength and increases the likelihood that the information sticks in that reader's long-term memory.

This is not about looking pretty. It is about presenting data in ways that align with how people see, think, and remember so that they can make more informed decisions and take action. These end goals are why we present our data in the first place.

Benefit 2: Adds to Credibility and Competence

The second benefit of effective data presentation continues to address the first criticism. Professional competence is communicated through consistent clarity in your dissemination. Inconsistent or unintentionally sloppy work reflects on the presenter. Even more subtle errors like slight misalignment or wordy slides leave the audience with a feeling of unease that translates onto the speaker, the report writer—you (Kosslyn, Kievit, Russell, & Shephard, 2012). On the other hand, effective choices about details like font and callout boxes boost perceptions of your legitimacy and professionalism. Design, ultimately, is fairly invisible. It works in the background, behind the solid research you conducted. It can undermine the quality of your study or enhance it in such a way that you get more attention as a result.

But it hinges on you knowing your key message—which is why this is not a skill you hand off to your department copyeditor or secretary. Only you, the one who posed the research questions and collected the data, know the key message you must convey.

Criticism: Design Is Expensive

Benefit 3: There Are Multiple Ways to Save Time

All that said, the second argument most often heard is that there is an insufficient budget to cover the time it takes to present data effectively. As we now know, it is less expensive to invest in design time before disseminating your work than to put weak work out in the world that wastes time and mental energy in the muddling and mucking of interpretation.

But, if you have been tallying as we moved along here, you probably realized that we often took extra steps to move away from some of the default settings in our software programs. I know this is beginning to sound time-consuming, especially given the length of a typical research report, multiplied by the number of report authors. So, here are two ways to save more time.

Style Sheets

Project managers in the graphic design world are effective people. They developed a system for streamlining the look and feel of a project from its very start through the use of style sheets. Style sheets are a record of conceptual graphic design–based decisions like gridwork dimensions, color palette, and font settings. These specifications are listed in one location, ranging from a page to an entire manual on branding guidelines, which serve as the code-book when designing a new document as part of a project. This way, when fresh staff are brought on to the project or additional data presentation products are created, then the decisions about color, graphics, arrangement, and type are already identified, and ongoing work blends with the project's research-based branding choices.

For some people, decisions about font choices and such are already dictated by your uni- versity or your department. If you are starting from scratch, make a plan and stick to it. What is your heading font? What are you going to use for your narrative text? How is your sidebar text spaced? Make these decisions as early as possible and then try very hard not to waver.

FIGURE 6.1   Style sheet for slideshow

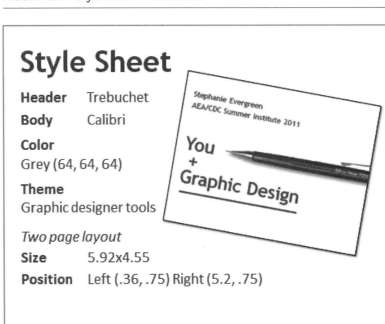

Here is one simple style sheet I created for my own slide decks. You can see that it names the fonts I chose for the headings and text of the slides, as well as the color of the text (including the RGB color code shown in parentheses to achieve that precise color). The bottom of the style sheet lists some helpful information. In this particular slideshow, I was demonstrating how to design research and evaluation reports, and thus many of my slides showed images of two report pages side-by-side. So, the specifications here in the style sheet identify the exact size and position for each of those example report page images so that I can ensure the images appear in a consistent location on every slide throughout the slide deck.

Importantly, the style sheet also displays a sample slide from the deck and details the nature of the additional imagery to include in the slides: graphic designer tools. In reality, it is better to be even more specific. Here are some of the questions I ask myself when considering images for the slide deck: Are the images real photographs or are illustrations okay? Is it better to include images of people actually holding graphic design tools so that the audience gets a sense of themselves in the work? Does the image background need to be white or some other color? Answering these questions from the beginning allows you to set up more specific image search parameters, and it saves probably 1 billion hours of your time.

FIGURE 6.2 Style sheet for Potent Presentations Initiative

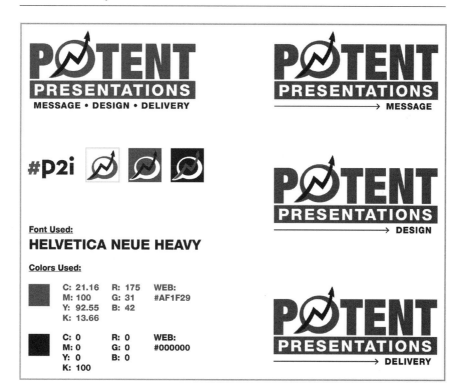

Source: © 2012 Reprinted with permission from the American Evaluation Association.

Here is another example from a project I led for the American Evaluation Association, called the Potent Presentations Initiative. At the very beginning of the project, we contracted with a graphic designer to produce a logo. In return, he provided us with the start of a style sheet. It displays the full logo, in the upper left, versions of the logo along the right for the occasions when I was speaking about one part of the initiative, and what some people refer to as "avatars"—those little square icons I can use as buttons, signifiers, and webpage tab identifiers. This sheet gives me a single source file I refer to each time I need to cut and paste a logo or an avatar. I accessed this page frequently throughout my work on this initiative.

Also notice that the designer made a stylized hashtag (with the # sign, for marking keywords on Twitter) because he knew we wanted to post our hashtag on our slides and handouts so that people could spread the message of the initiative. The graphic designer listed the color codes he used, in CMYK, RGB, and web, which allowed us to construct a broader palette from those colors if we needed to. He also identified the font he used in creating the logo.

On your own project style sheets, you probably need to specify a larger set of variations on these fonts to fit your needs. For a project that included dissemination both by paper and slideshow, Figure 6.3 is an example of the minimum decisions you want to make, and how to display them in a style sheet.

FIGURE 6.3   Paper font styles

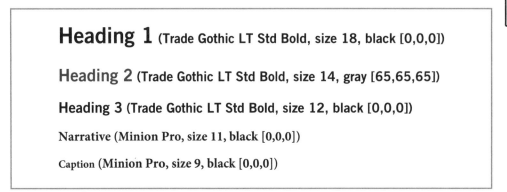

FIGURE 6.4   Slideshow font styles

You might decide to add in a particular font specification for a sidebar, a callout, or an alternative text font for your slideshow.

Making these decisions near the beginning of the project increases efficiency by streamlining the design. The few times I consulted with organizations and delightfully discovered they were using style sheets, I found the style sheets did not go into enough detail. It might seem to lean a bit toward micromanagement, but a lack of sufficient specification in the style guide leaves gaps that cause confusion, among both the teammates designing the effective data presentations and the readers who have to mentally reconcile meaningless style changes.

What If a Client or Funder Has a Style Guide?

Even though you have taken care to make nuanced design decisions, in some consulting situations, the client has his or her own branding. Should you assume this branding or keep your own? Well, it depends. If the client needs you to come in with strong consulting, maybe to help change the minds of reluctant staff, using your own branding can be helpful. If the client needs your work to appear more like something he or she adopted, defer to that branding and style guide. And then you have grayer areas like this: Say your department wins a grant from a large state agency, which insists all grantees follow their style guide. But it is incomplete. Insert your own branding and style decisions where there are gaps. Perhaps you can use your own department's color palette on the graphs or your own font choices in a report sidebar. Of course, check that the style guides play somewhat nicely with one another so that the report does not look schizophrenic. In other words, be flexible. Advance your own style guide where you can and defer to others when necessary.

Indeed this was one of the main flaws I saw in the multitude of reports I reviewed for my dissertation. A section change occurred, and suddenly there were new fonts, new color schemes, and so on. On top of needlessly causing confusion for the readers, it also reflects poorly on the writers as well. Style sheets ensure consistency even when there are multiple people working on a project or paper, and they are especially helpful when you have long-term projects and personnel changes.

Sample style sheets are included online, where you can download the template and fill in your own details.

Save Themes

Once you specify your font, spacing, color, justification, and so forth, save your decisions. Over and above the efficiency of developing a style guide, you can streamline one step further by saving these settings directly into your software program.

First, you modify the settings according to your style guide using the *Styles* in the upper right of the ribbon bar in Word.

FIGURE 6.5 Screenshot depicting where to adjust settings according to your style sheet

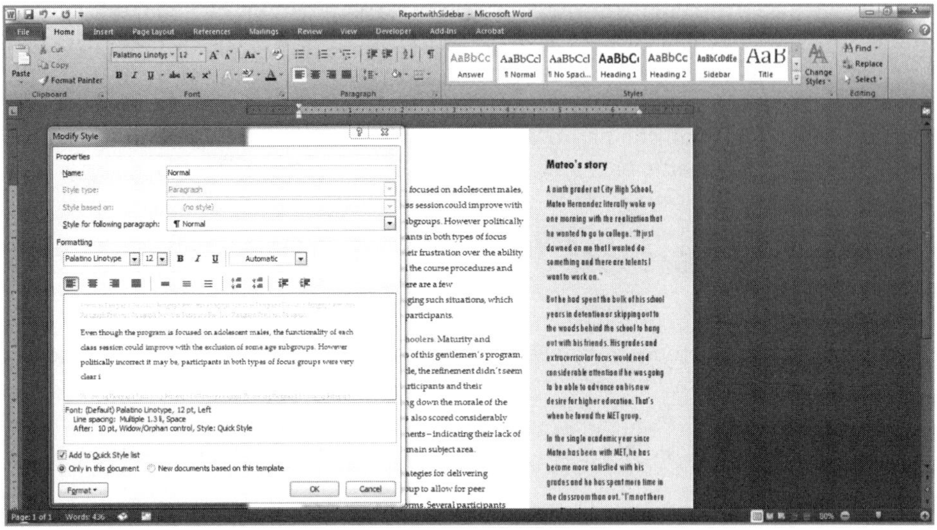

You right-click on *Normal* from the *Styles* options and then click *Modify* from the menu. That opens the dialogue box shown here. From this box, select your preferences to align with the decisions you made about how you want the narrative text to look. Repeat this process for your headings, sidebars, and whatever other text styles you've chosen.

Once those settings are in place within the Styles group, click on the *Page Layout* tab.

FIGURE 6.6 Screenshot showing how to save style sheet settings

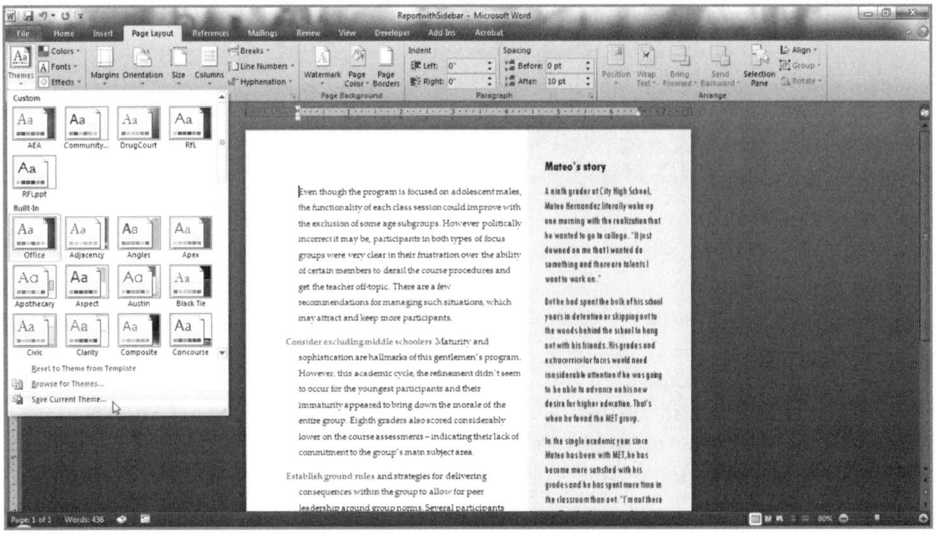

Over in the *Themes* group, click on the little arrow under the Themes icon. Head to the bottom and click on *Save Theme,* and name that theme after your project. This allows you to retain all of the decisions you just made for the future. Those same options are then available whenever you open any of the other Microsoft programs on your computer. You can see from the screenshot that I have gone through this process many times—these are all shown under Custom themes. To help me keep things sorted, I tend to create a new style guide for each of my projects. The bonus is that when you ship your document to your colleague or classmate, all she has to do is click on *Save Theme* on her computer and the reporting is made more efficient for her as well.

KEY POINTS TO REMEMBER

As long as you can keep these points in mind, you have all the reason you need to go forth presenting data effectively:

- Graphics, font, color, and placement matter to the brains and memory of your readers.

- A small investment of time upfront to make style decisions increases efficiency throughout the project.

- Document design decisions on a style sheet that serves as a reference point throughout your project.

- After setting up your design decisions in your first document, save the settings as a theme so that you do not have to establish those settings in the future.

- Proper and consistent use of these design principles makes your data presentation clearer and better understood.

- In order to emphasize key content and present it effectively, you must carefully think through and identify your key content, tapping in to input from other classmates or colleagues cognitively close to the data.

HOW CAN I EXTEND THIS?

Check Out

Head over to the *Guardian's* website on data visualization, Datablog (http://www.guardian .co.uk/news/datablog)—Click on any of the headlines to view their interactive visualizations, something not really discussed in this book. Play with the interactivity a bit. Their work is high quality, but improvements could be made. What would you suggest? The raw data file behind each visualization is usually available for download, too. So you can demonstrate your recommendations and create your own graphs.

Navigate to the web companion for this book (www.sage.com/evergreen)—There you will find even more examples of effective data presentation. I posted directions and short video tutorials for replicating some of the processes I describe in this book using alternative, free software and the latest version of Microsoft Office. You can also find my blog, where I keep you up to date on the most effective data presentation.

Try This

After viewing the interactive visualizations at the *Guardian's* Datablog, grab a paper copy of *USA Today* (their online stories often do not include the graphs they print). Compare the data visualization styles of the two news agencies. Verbalize how the differences in style send different messages to the reader. What are the messages you pick up, not from the story itself, but from the stylistic decisions the designers made?

Develop a style sheet for one of your papers or slideshows. Write out the fonts, colors, imagery, and sizes you decide to use. Review the Research and Evaluation Report Layout Checklist located in the Appendix and downloadable online to guide your design decisions.

WHERE CAN I GO FOR MORE INFORMATION?

Kosslyn, S. M., Kievit, R. A., Russell, A. G., & Shephard, J. M. (2012). PowerPoint presentation flaws and failures: A psychological analysis. *Frontiers in Psychology, 3*(230), 1–22.

Research and Evaluation Report Layout Checklist

This checklist was originally a product of my dissertation—which means it is built on an almost torturous amount of peer-reviewed research. Additionally, I pulled together a panel of graphic design experts who further modified these checkpoints. Then, I had a group of 16 researchers and evaluators pilot the instrument on a sample of evaluation reports, which fine-tuned a few more pieces here and there. It has since been distributed and downloaded thousands of times. The guiding ideas in each section served as the framework for this book.

You can use the checklist in several ways:

1. Before report writing, to plan formatting and layout, which influences the content in that you might decide to use sidebars or callout boxes to highlight key parts of your text. In this case, you do not necessarily need the scoring mechanism included in the checklist.

2. After report writing, to assess the extent to which you used graphic design principles to organize and emphasize your data presentation. In this instance, the scoring feature of the checklist is helpful.

3. On the reports of your colleagues and classmates, to determine how well they integrate graphic design to support their reporting. Here again, scoring the report can be useful.

While the title refers to written reports, nearly all of the guidance is equally applicable to other methods of data presentation, as exemplified throughout this book. Review the checkpoints and guidance found below and then visit this book's website (www.sagepub.com/evergreen) to download a copy of the checklist to share.

Research and Evaluation Report Layout Checklist

by Stephanie D. H. Evergreen, PhD

This checklist is meant to be used as a diagnostic guide to identify elements of evaluation reports that can be enhanced using graphic design best practices and/or the assistance of a graphic design expert. Suggestions are best suited for those using standard Microsoft Word software.

Instructions

Rate each aspect of the report using the following rubric, by circling the most appropriate letter. Use the Best Practice section as a guide for improvement.

F = Fully Met,   P = Partly Met,   N = Not Met

Type	Rating	Best Practice	Notes
Text fonts are used for narrative text	F P N	Use serif fonts. Nothing with lots of graphic detail.	*Nice serif choices* include Garamond, Palatino, Cambria
Long reading is in 9- to 11-point size	F P N	Studies have shown that 11-point text is easiest to read at length, but it depends on the typeface (font).	*Nice sans serif choices* are Trebuchet, Verdana, Calibri
Body text has stylistic uniformity	F P N	Each text section has normal text in sentence case (no bold, no all caps), except in short areas of intentional emphasis. This supports undistracted reading.	*Sentence case* is when the first letter of the line is capitalized and all others are lowercase, except proper nouns.
Line spacing is 11 to 13 points	F P N	For lines within a paragraph, generally choose 1–2 points larger than the size of the body text.	*Body text* is what comprises the narrative of the report.
Headers and callouts are emphasized	F P N	Header should be 150–200% of body text size. Sans serif or decorative is okay. Use sentence case. Contrast with body text by using different size, style, and/or color. Too similar looks unintentional.	By contrast, *header text* is what makes up your headlines and titles, also known as display text.
No more than three fonts are used	F P N	A change in font indicates a change in meaning. Use font changes to guide the reader through information according to importance.	● Default bullet size (too big)
Bullets are slightly less thick than text	F P N	If bullets must be used, decrease their size to slightly less (70–80%) than the point size of the font. Otherwise, they are too strong and distracting. If good spacing is used in lieu of bullets, this best practice is Fully Met.	• Appropriate bullet size

Arrangement	Rating	Best Practice	Notes
Alignment is consistent	F P N	Alignment is an early attention feature easily noticed by a reader, so be sure that elements start in the same place on each page unless misaligned on purpose. Avoid centered elements.	*Imagine each page* divided into rows and columns. Draw imaginary lines to check that elements are aligned at the start of each row and at the top of each column.
Columns are 8 to 12 words in length	F P N	This is 50–80 characters, depending on font. Longer is difficult to track from line to line, shorter creates too many hyphenated words, distracting the reader. See?	*Asymmetry* is an easy way to create interest. Try placing a cool picture off to one side of the page.
Important elements are prominent	F P N	Most prominent position is top half of page and/or emphasized by size, color, orientation, etc. Supportive information is toned down.	*Wide margins* are a quick way to create empty area and manage line length.
Body text is left or full justified	F P N	Ragged right edge is more informal but easier to read for average readers. Full justification is formal, easier for fluent readers, but creates design issues with "white rivers" or large gaps of white space between words.	
Grouped items logically belong together	F P N	Grouped items are interpreted as one chunk. Place logical items together. Add space between groups. Minimize space between header and body text.	
Empty area is allocated on each page	F P N	Leave plenty of space between paragraphs, around page margins, and between text and graphics. It gives eyes a rest.	

Graphics	Rating	Best Practice	Notes
Pictures/graphic elements are present	F P N	Multimode learning increases chance of information storage in long-term memory because it eases cognitive load of body text. Choose pictures or graphics related to your topic. Graphics include, but should not be limited to, tables and charts. If there are no graphics, this section is scored as Not Met.	*Pictures and graphics* related to your content make your content more memorable. *Choose pictures* from quality sources, such as paid websites. Watermarks or fuzzy images are signs of an amateur. *Use a cover page* at the beginning of a report. This is a good place for a very large graphic.
Graphics are near associated text	F P N	If readers must flip around to interpret between text and graphic, comprehension is impaired.	
Graphics are simple	F P N	Less visual noise leads to better assimilation. Eliminate gradation, textures, or graphics as backgrounds. Segment complex graphics into smaller chunks.	
Size corresponds to changes in meaning	F P N	Use, for example, larger pictures on chapter start pages. In graphing, for example, be sure the height of columns proportionately represents data.	
Graphics direct toward text	F P N	Use the power of an image to direct the reader's gaze from the image to the associated text. Eyes in a photo, for example, should look inward at the text.	
Visual theme is evident	F P N	Pick a visual theme that can be used in different forms throughout reporting to give strong emotional connection.	
Some elements are repeated	F P N	Repetition of some graphic elements adds unity to the piece and makes work more memorable. Be careful not to overdo it—too many elements can add clutter or complication.	

Color	Rating	Best Practice	Notes
Narrative text is dark gray or black	F P N	Black has highest comprehension levels, with low intensity colors taking a distant second place.	Keep in mind various culture-laden *color connotations*. For example, pink is highly associated with feminine qualities in the United States. Make sure your color choices are appropriate for your audience.
Background has white/subdued color	F P N	Reversed-out text (e.g., white text on black background) slightly impairs information retention.	
One or two emphasis colors are used	F P N	Subdued colors that still contrast with the background should be used. When used, it should be to actually emphasize important information like data in a graph. If more than one is selected, consider choosing along a color gradation so that order of importance is implicit.	Note that *people with colorblindness* have difficulty with red-green and yellow-blue combinations.
Color changes denote meaning changes	F P N	Color changes signal a change in hierarchy of information. Be intentional with color changes so that a viewer doesn't get confused.	A safe bet is *to use your client's colors.*
Color reprints legibly in black and white	F P N	Color looks different on a computer screen than on paper. Print on a black-and-white printer and then make a copy of that printout to check legibility.	

Time to add up your points: _____

F = 1 point

P = ½ point

N = 0 points

Well-formatted reports score within 23 to 25 points. At this score, report readers are better able to read and retain content.

177

Index

NOTE: Page numbers referring to figures are followed by (fig.).